WIRE WEAVING

*Beginner's Guide + Intermediate Guide
+ Chain Maille + Kumihimo Wirework*

TABLE OF CONTENTS

WIRE WEAVING FOR BEGINNERS

*Make Your First Wire Jewelry Project
and Learn Basic Skills*

INTRODUCTION

The art of wire weaving has been around since ancient times. Archeologists have found wire woven accessory dating back as early as 1446 BC. There have been pieces of wire jewelry found in the tombs of ancient pharaohs as well. This type of accessory does not require casting or soldering or even fire to create it; that's why the ancient civilization adopted it.

Gold was one of the first metals to be used for wire jewelry. It was not too hard to pound into sheets with a hammer before being cut and rolled into strips.

The art of making wire jewelry involves bending and twisting wires to create beautiful shapes on their own or with beads, stones, or gems. Wire manipulation takes place after cutting it to the desired length and then flattening it with pliers. This is all done with no glue, solder, or anything else — just different strength of wires supporting each other by their design.

Wire weaving has been passed down from one generation to another. Being knowledgeable about the craft's history is just as important as learning different weaves. History keeps the art alive, after all. Knowing that most of the designs are based on some ancient ones adds an air of elegance, tradition, and class to it.

Wire weaving is not as difficult as it looks. All it takes are good tools, proper wires, and practice. There are a few wire types to choose from which can be complemented with beautiful stones and beads and woven into gorgeous pieces. Once you have mastered the basic weaves and grasped the techniques, you can start crafting your own magnificent jewelry.

This guide covers the wire and tools that you need to begin with, as well as some of the basic weaves and weaving techniques. Follow the simple three projects included in this book and make some classically beautiful jewelry items that you can wear or gift with pride. There are helpful hints and tips throughout the guide to make sure you get the best start to your new craft, too.

CHAPTER 1: TOOLS

As you become more advanced in the art of wire weaving, you may find yourself having to buy various tools for some of the fancier designs. As a beginner, choosing tools to start with can be perplexing. There are so many types out there to choose from, and each one has its own interesting use.

When starting out, go with the basics first and complete some simple wire weaving projects before splashing out on the more expensive wires, tools, and gadgets.

The items listed below are required for the simple wire weaving projects in this guide. As long as you have them, you will be able to follow along later.

Wire

For weave and technique practice in this tutorial, you will need:

- 1 x 13.7 M (15 YD) spool length pack- 20 Gauge Copper Wire
- 1 x 36.5 M (40YD) spool length pack - 28 Gauge Copper Wire

When creating jewelry with wire, you will come across wires in various types, colors, shapes, and sizes. Don't twist yourself in knots about the huge selection on offer for this tutorial, though, since the actual wire needed is listed with each project.

Under "Handy Tips for Wire Weaving," there is a section on the different wire types, gauges, and temper. There is also a conversion table available to help you convert gauge to millimeters and inches.

Chain Nose Pliers

There are many kinds of pliers to choose from. Most of them will come in handy when you move on to more intricate projects.

For the sake of this tutorial, though, we will only be needing the **chain nose pliers**. It is the most versatile type and can be used on every application. They are great for flattening ends, adjusting tensions, and looping wires. You should always have one in your wire weaving tool kit.

Flush Cutters

Each type of cutter has its own use for various wire types. For aluminum wire and softer copper wire that is 20 gauge or lower, for instance, the flush cutter is recommended. That is also what we will use for the weave examples.

CHAPTER 2: WEAVES

Different types of weaves can either be basic or complex. As your creativity grows, you can begin to experiment and design your own weaves.

To see the difference between the base wires and the weaving wire, the weaves have been done in silver for the base wires and copper for the weaving wire.

As you will be working with more than one base wire at a time, we will be labeling them as BW1, BW2, BW3, etc. BW1 will always be your starting base wire, BW2 will be the second base wire, and so on.

Here are five basic stitches that can become the foundation of some intricate patterns.

Starting the Weaves

For the following weaves, you will need to cut your base wires and weaving wire. Some of the weaves will need two base wires while others may require three, but all the base and weaving wires are the same size.

For the Base Wires:

- Use the 20-gauge wire.
- Cut each base wire to 70 mm (0.04 in.).
- Each pattern will have how many base wires will be needed for that particular weave.

For the Weaving Wire:

- Use the 28 gauge wire.
- Cut the weaving wire to 150 mm (5.91 in.).

Working With the Wire:

- Wear protective glasses to protect your eyes against any metal pieces that may spring up while cutting the wire and from the weaving tail.
- If you find it hard to hold the base wires, you can use a ring clamp to securely hold the pieces while weaving.
- If you need to tighten up the weaving pattern, try to squish the wires together with your fingers first. Unless you have a plastic-tipped wire straightener, other tools will damage the wire.
- As the weaves are quite small, you may find it more comfortable to use a magnifying glass to weave under.
- Always make sure that there is enough light when you are working with the wire to prevent eye problems and see the weave pattern well.

Two-Wire Figure Eight

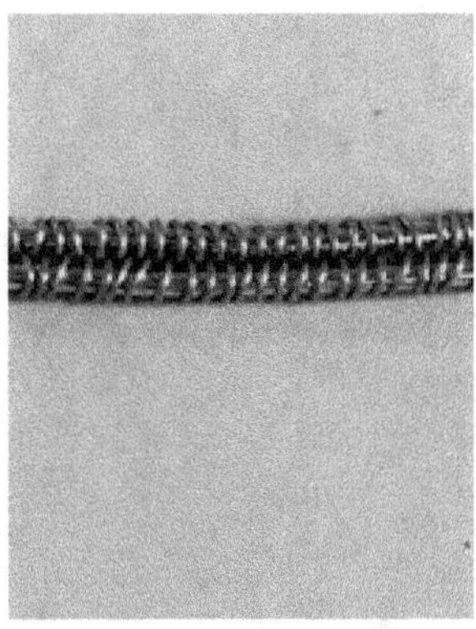

1. Cut two pieces of base wire (BW1 and BW2).
2. Cut one piece of weaving wire.
3. For this weave, BW1 will be the top base wire and BW2 will be the bottom base wire.
4. Holding BW1 horizontally, position the weaving wire vertically against BW1 leaving a small tail at the bottom. The tail should be long enough to make a small loop when you are done with the pattern to finish off the piece.

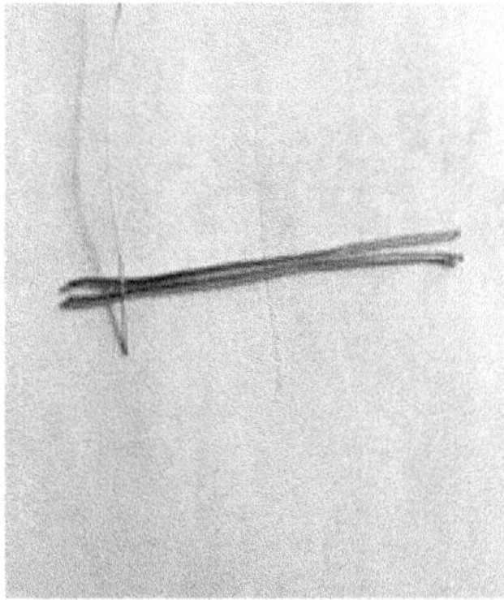

5. It is a bit tricky to keep this loop in place. To anchor it, form a solid loop by bending the weaving wire tailpiece around the BW1 as shown in the picture below. Bring the weaving wire through the middle of BW1 and Bw2, pulling over the front of BW2.

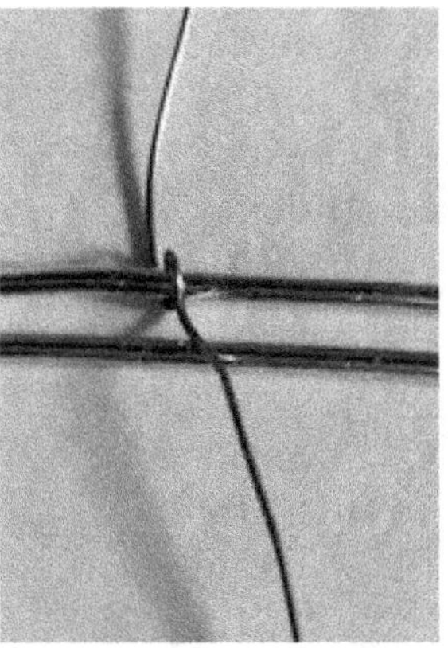

6. Create a loop over BW2 by pulling the weaving wire over the front of BW2 and then up and around the back of the wire. Keep the loop stable by placing a finger on the bottom of the BW2 loop.

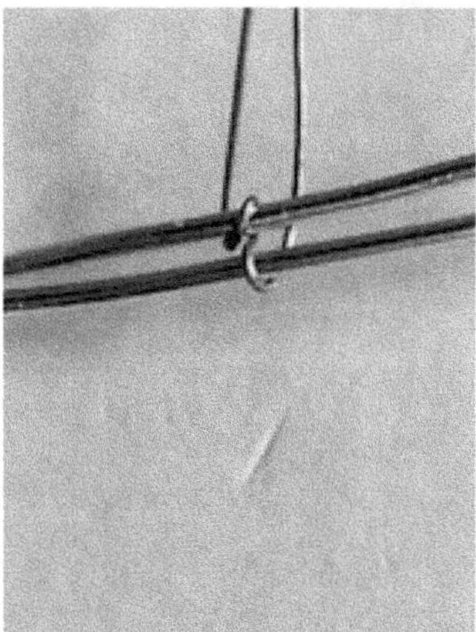

7. Holding the bottom of the loop around BW2, pass the weaving wire through the middle of BW1 and BW2 and then pull the weaving wire over the top and around the back of BW1. After that, pull the weaving wire through the middle of BW1 and BW2.

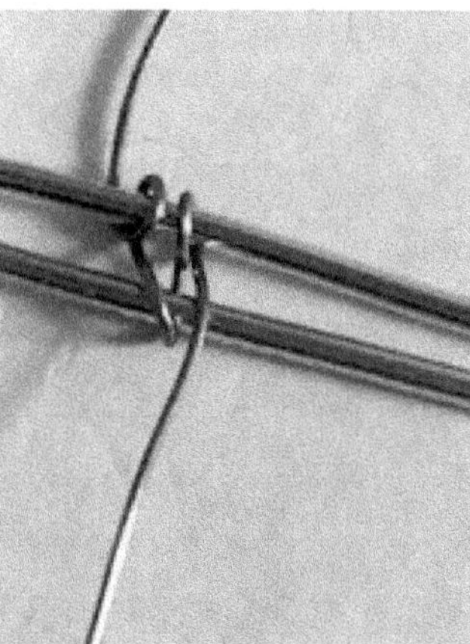

8. Repeat steps #7 and #8, respectively. Remember to squish your loops together to make them flush and tight. The weaving pattern will start to look like the picture below only when your weave is a little tighter.

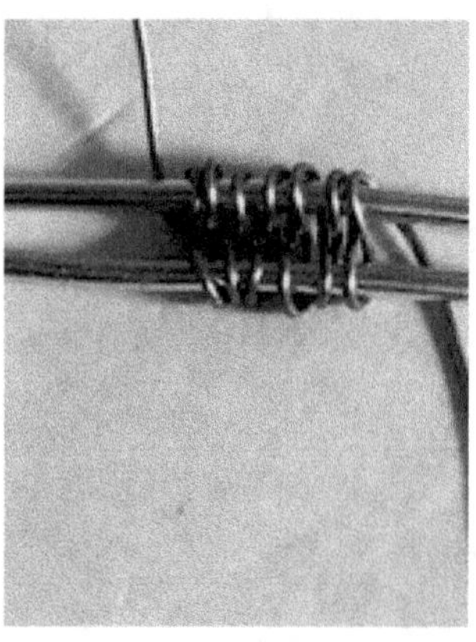

9. Repeat the pattern until you are close to the end of the base wires, leaving 5 mm (0.2 in.) free at the end of the base wires.

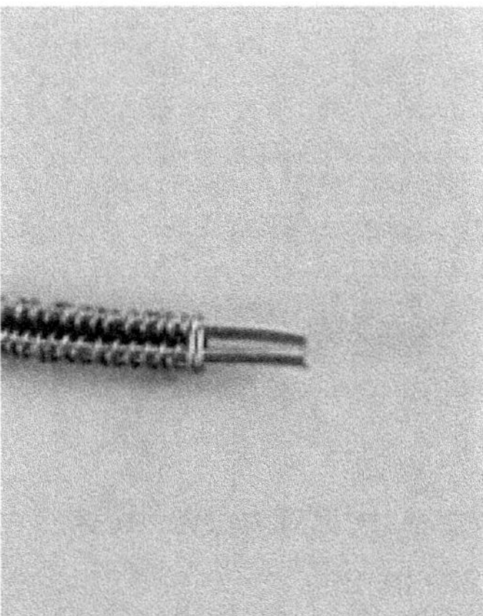

10. Finish off the weave by following the procedure in the last section of this chapter. Put the finished piece in a safe place so that you can use it later.

Two-Wire Weave

Zigzag Pattern

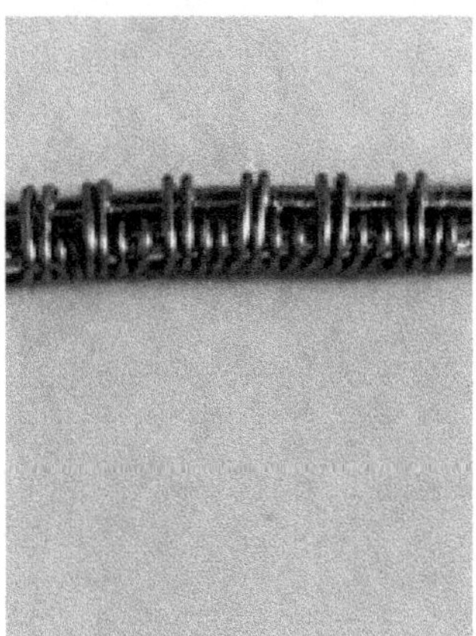

1. Cut two pieces of base wire (BW1 and BW2).
2. Cut one piece of weaving wire.
3. For this weave, BW1 will be the bottom base wire and BW2 will be the top base wire.
4. Holding BW1 horizontally, position the weaving wire vertically against BW1 leaving a small tail at the top. The tail should be long enough to make a small loop when you are done with the pattern to finish off the piece.

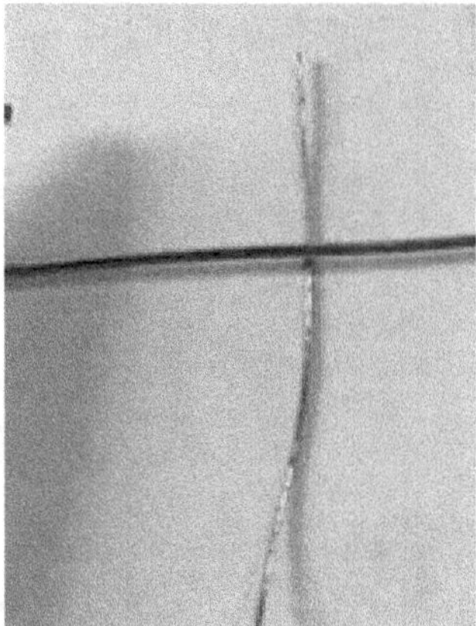

5. Using the longer part of the weaving wire, wrap two loops around BW1. Pull the weaving wire up and over the front of BW1 and make two loops.

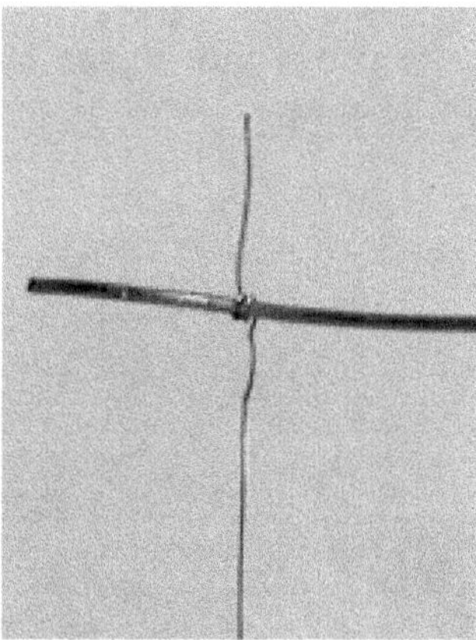

6. Take BW2 and hold it horizontally above BW1.

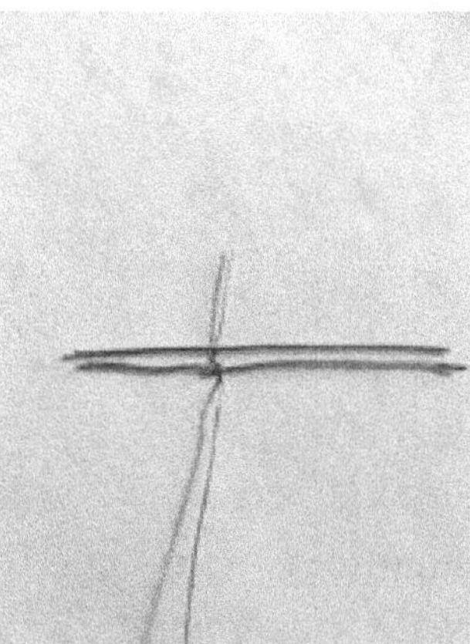

7. Using the longer part of the weaving wire, make two loops over both base wires by pulling the weaving wire up and over the front of BW1 and then continue up and over BW2. Repeat this loop to make two loops.

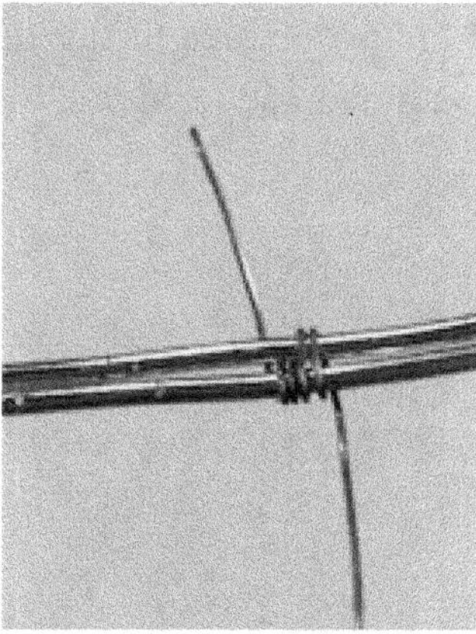

8. Take a weaving wire and loop it twice around the top frame, ending with the wire behind the frames and hanging below the bottom frame wire.

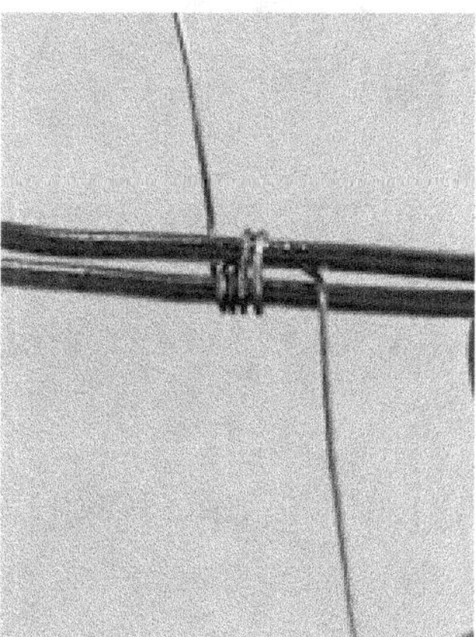

9. Repeat step #7.
10. Repeat step #8.
11. Repeat the pattern until you are close to the end of the base wires, leaving 5 mm (0.2 in.) free at the end of the base wires.

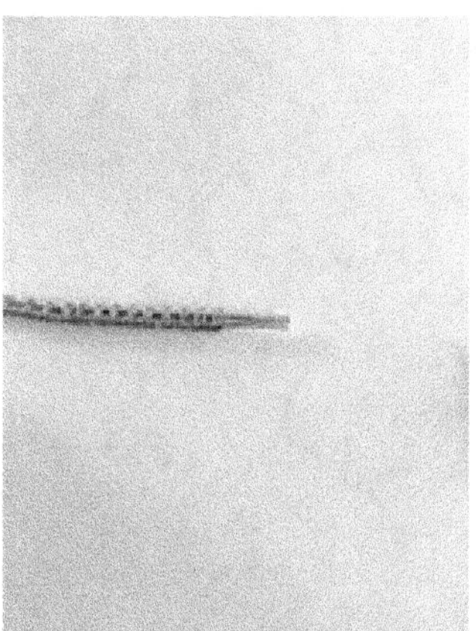

12. Finish off the weave by following the procedure in the last section of this chapter. Put the finished weave piece in a safe place so that you can use it later.

Basic Basket Weave

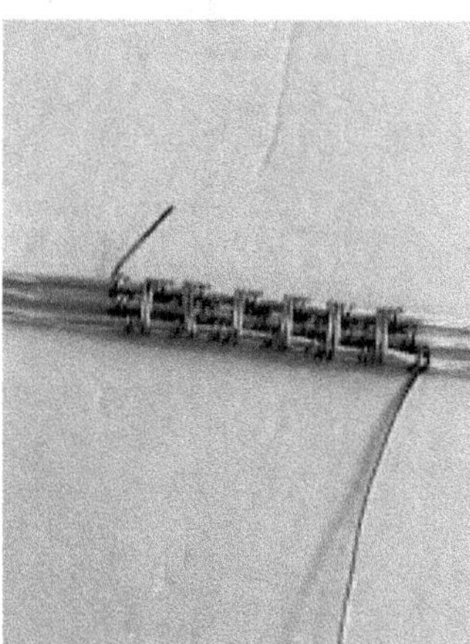

The basket weave has many variations. In truth, you can incorporate up to five base wires to make one. For this particular box basket weave, however, you will only use three base wires, which is a good start for beginners. You do not want to try controlling more wires than that while learning different weaves.

1. Cut three pieces of base wire (BW1, BW2, and BW3).

2. Cut one piece of weaving wire.

3. For this weave, BW1 will be the top base wire, BW2 will be the middle base wire, and BW3 will be the bottom base wire.

4. Holding BW1 horizontally, position the weaving wire vertically against BW1 leaving a small tail at the bottom. The tail should be long enough to make a small loop when you are done with the pattern to finish off the piece.

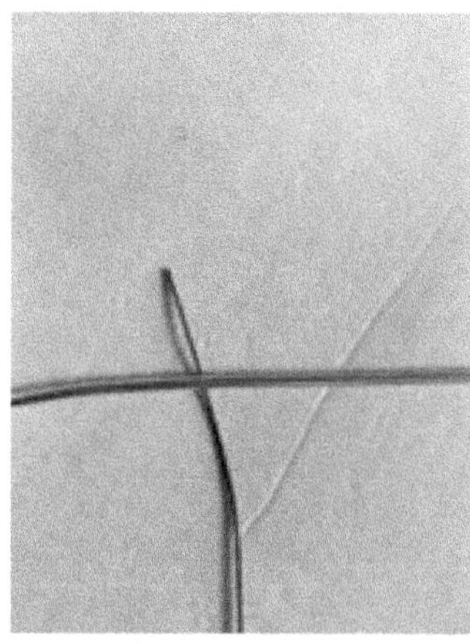

5. Using the longer part of the weaving wire, wrap two loops around BW1. Pull the weaving wire up and over the front of BW1 and make two loops.

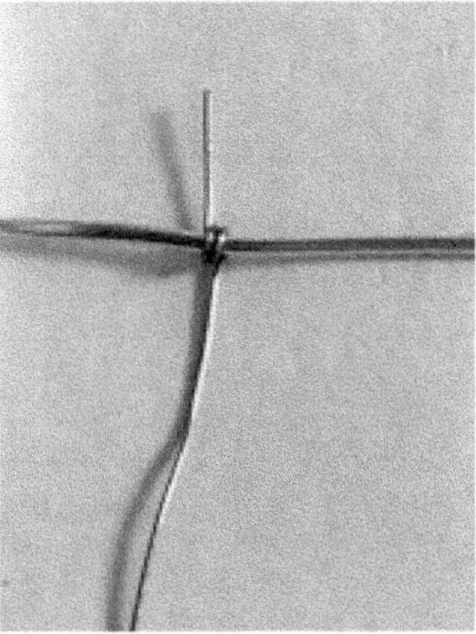

6. Take BW2 and hold it horizontally below BW1.

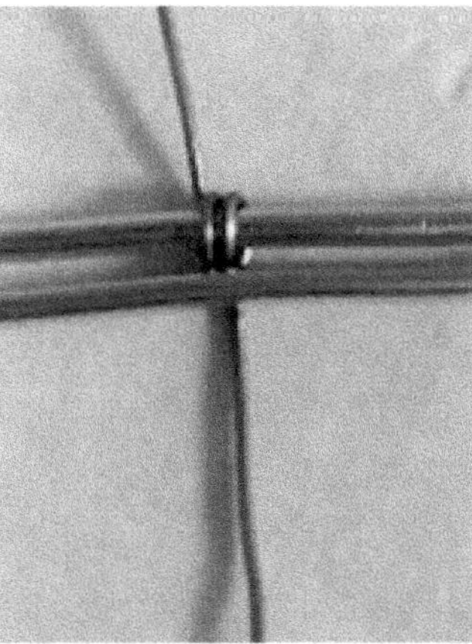

7. Create two loops around BW2 by pulling the weaving wire up and around the bottom of BW2 and then through the middle of BW1 and Bw2, repeating this loop to create two loops around BW2.

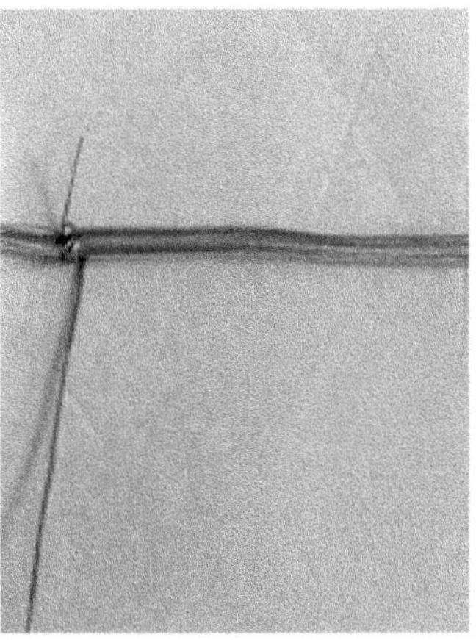

8. Take BW3 and hold it horizontally below BW2.

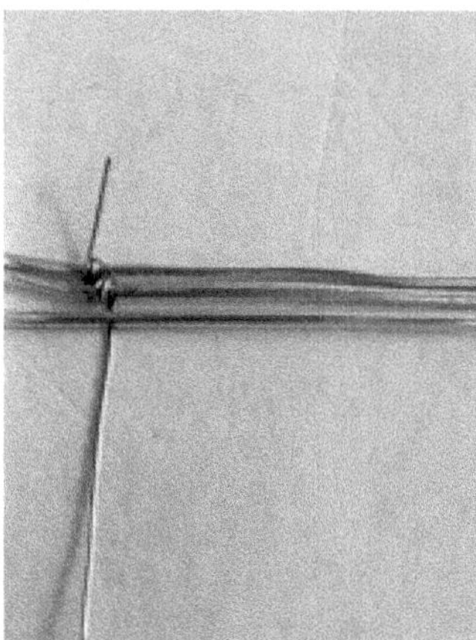

9. Create two loops around BW3 by pulling the weaving wire up and around the bottom of BW3 and then through the middle of BW2 and Bw3, repeating this loop to create two loops around BW3.

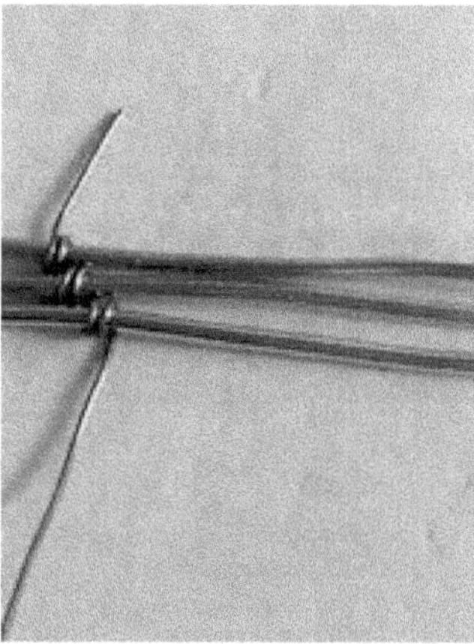

10. Create two loops with the weaving wire around all three base wires from BW3, over BW2, and then around and over BW1. Repeat the loop a second time to create two loops.

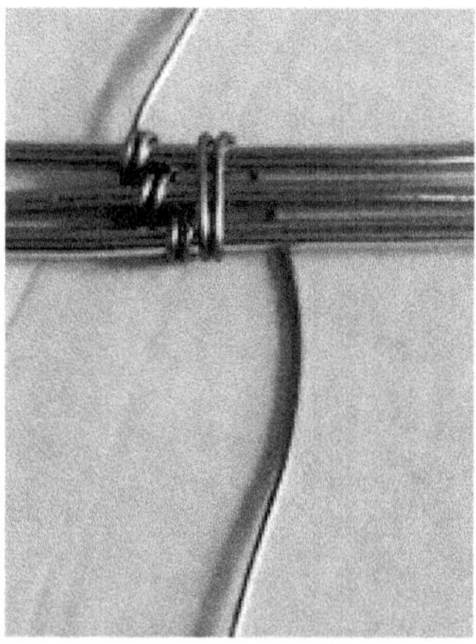

11. Repeat steps 5, 7, 9, and 10, respectively.

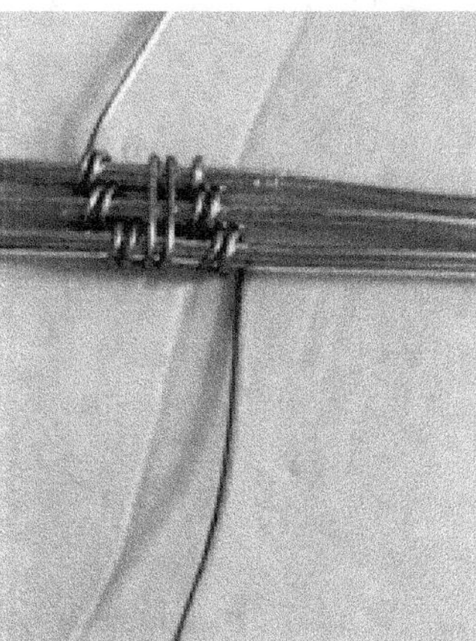

12. Repeat the pattern until you are close to the end of the base wires, leaving 5 mm (0.2 in.) free at the end of the base wires.

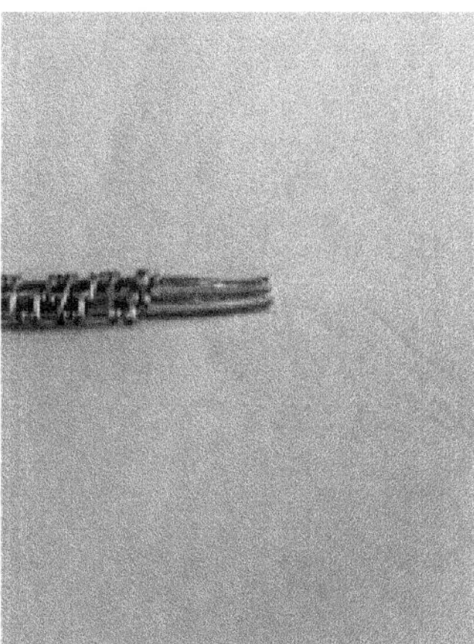

13. Finish off the weave by following the procedure in the last section of this chapter. Put the finished weave piece in a safe place so that you can use it later.

Snake Weave

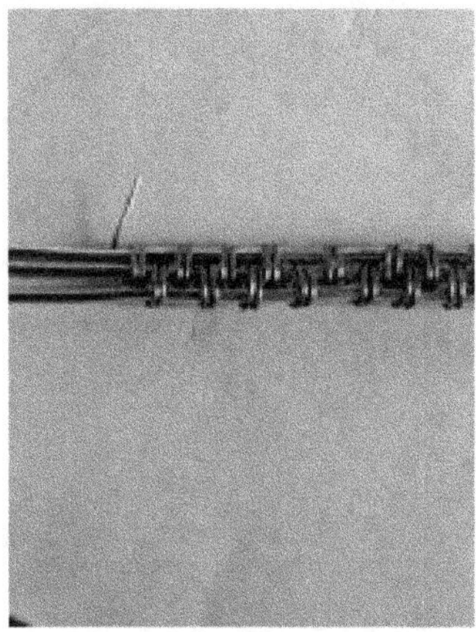

The snake weave is a handy pattern that can be used to make a nice simple bracelet or wrist cuff. Similar to the previous weave, it can have a few base wires. However, for this tutorial, you will only use three base wires.

1. Cut three pieces of base wire (BW1, BW2, and BW3).
2. Cut one piece of weaving wire.
3. For this weave, BW1 will be the top base wire, BW2 will be the middle base wire, and BW3 will be the bottom base wire.
4. Holding BW1 and BW2 horizontally, position the weaving wire vertically at the back of both BW1 and BW2, leave a small tail at the top. The tail should be long enough to make a small loop when you are done with the pattern to finish off the piece. Make two loops around both BW2 and BW1 by pulling the weaving wire up around the bottom of BW2 and then over and around the back of BW1. Repeat the loop a second time to make two loops.

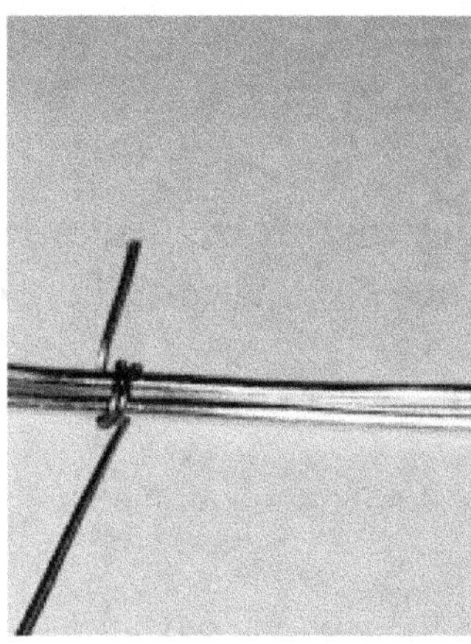

5. Take BW3 and hold it horizontally below BW2.

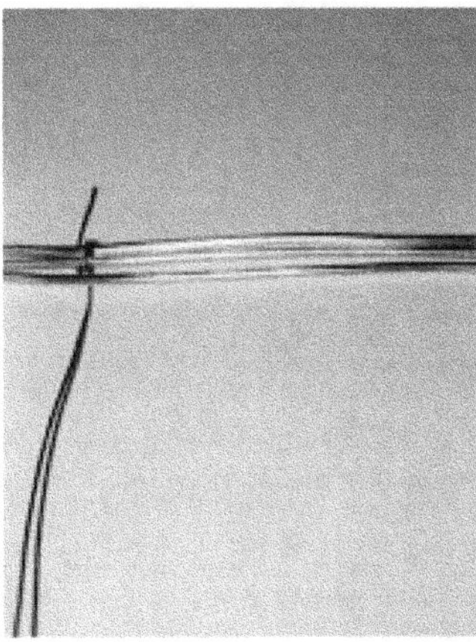

6. Make two loops around both BW3 and BW2 by pulling the weaving wire up around the bottom of BW2 and then pushing the weaving wire in between BW1 and BW2. Pull the wire back down towards BW2 and repeat the loop to make two loops around BW2 and BW3.

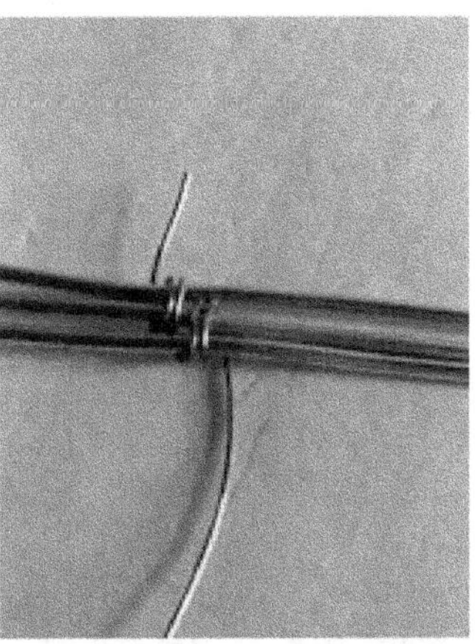

7. Make two loops around both BW2 and BW1 by pulling the weaving wire up around the bottom of BW2 around the back of BW1. Pull the weaving wire down over the front of BW1 and push it in between BW2 and BW3 to create a loop around BW1 and BW2. Repeat the loop a second time to make two loops.

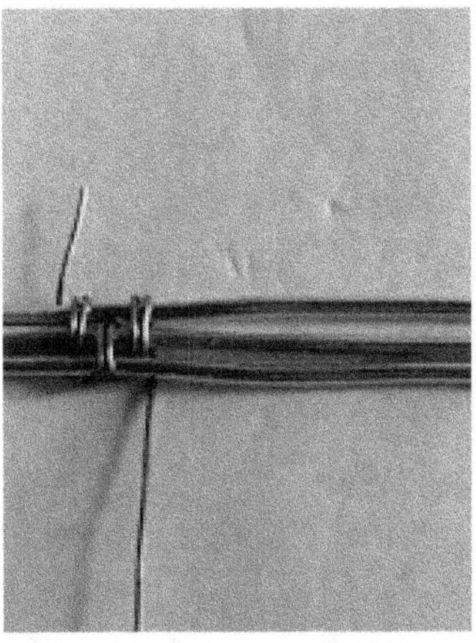

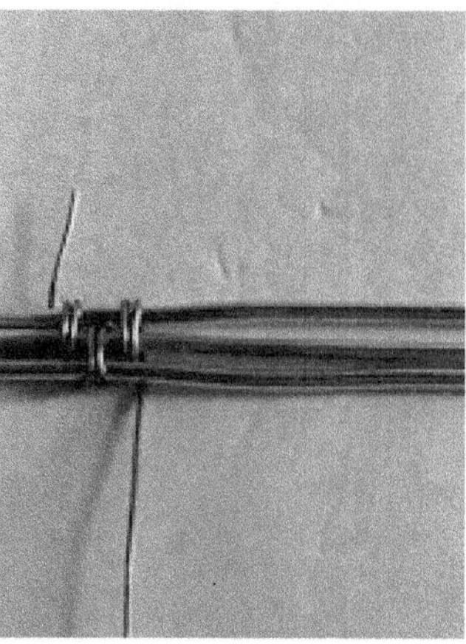

8. Repeat steps #6 and #7.
9. Repeat the pattern until you are close to the end of the base wires, leaving 5 mm (0.2 in.) free at the end of the base wires.

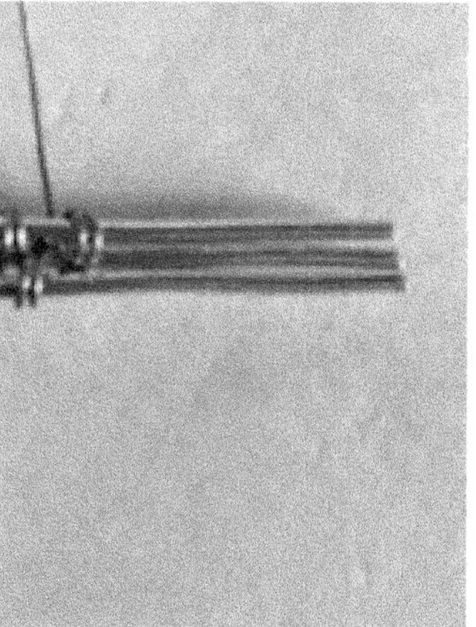

10. If you have done the previous weaves, you should know how to finish off the weave. If not, go to the last section of the chapter "Finishing Off the Weave" to neaten up the piece.
11. Put the weave aside so that you can use it later.

Flame Stitch

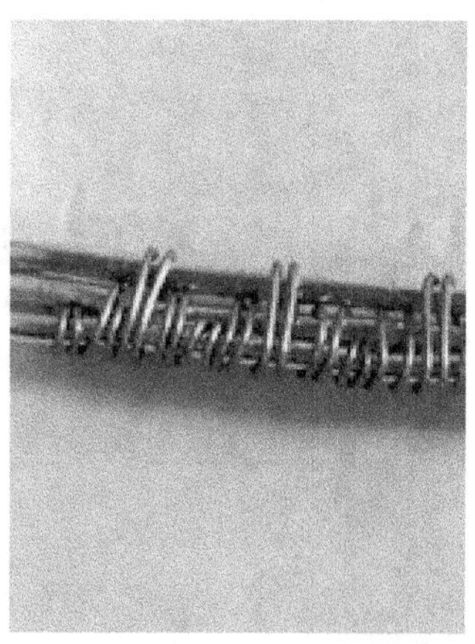

This is an easy variation of the flame stitch. Using three base wires, it is a great stitch to start learning how to work with 3 frame or base wires.

1. Cut three pieces of base wire (BW1, BW2, and BW3).
2. Cut one piece of weaving wire.
3. For this weave, BW1 will be the bottom base wire, BW2 will be the middle base wire, and BW3 will be the top base wire.
4. Holding BW1 horizontally, position the weaving wire vertically at the back of BW1, leaving a small tail at the top. The tail should be long enough to make a small loop when you are done with the pattern to finish off the piece.

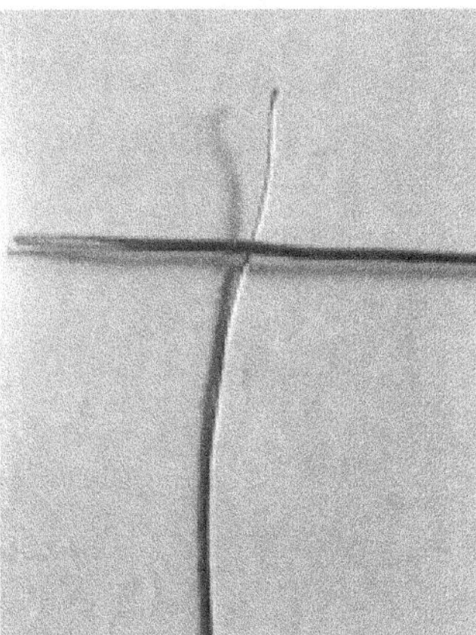

5. Make two loops around BW1 by pulling the weaving wire up around the bottom and then over and around its back. Repeat the loop a second time to make two loops.

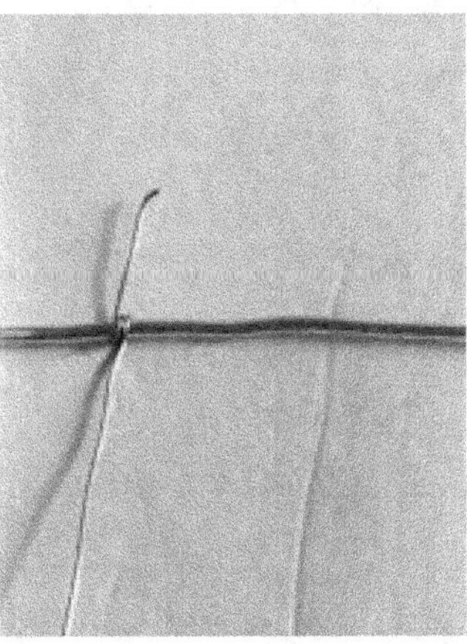

6. Take BW2 and hold it horizontally above BW1.

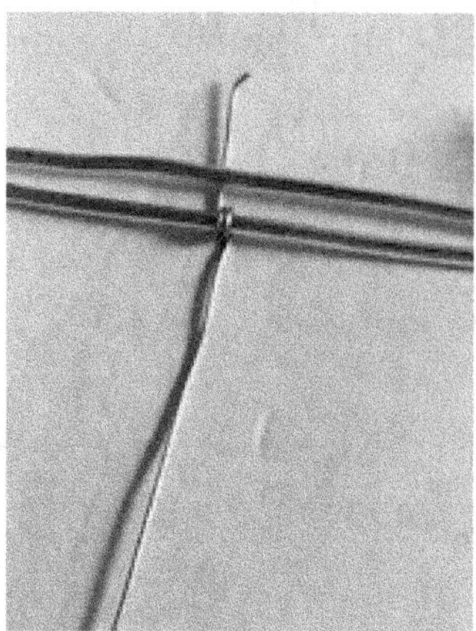

7. Take the weaving wire and make two loops over both BW2 and BW1. Pull the wire up and over the front of both BW2 and BW1, respectively. Pull the wire back down and repeat the loop to make two loops around BW2 and BW1.

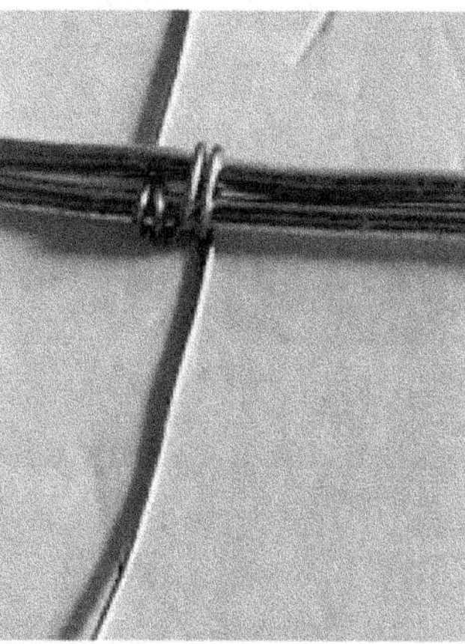

8. Take BW3 and hold it horizontally above BW2.

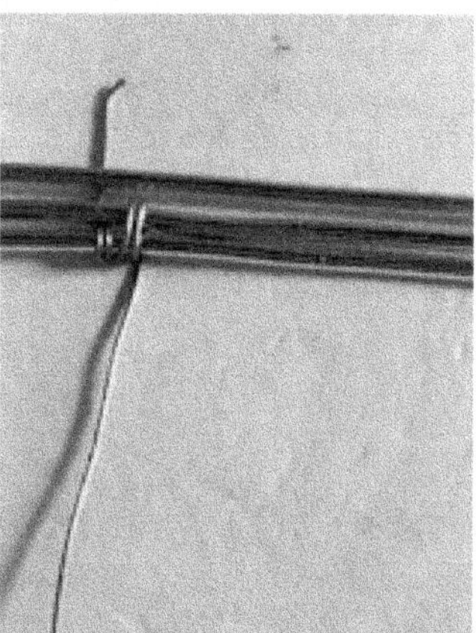

9. Take the weaving wire and make two loops around BW3, BW2, and BW1. Pull the weaving wire up around the front of BW3, BW2, and BW1 and then loop it around the three base wires following the same loop to create two loops around all three base wires (BW3, BW2, and BW1).

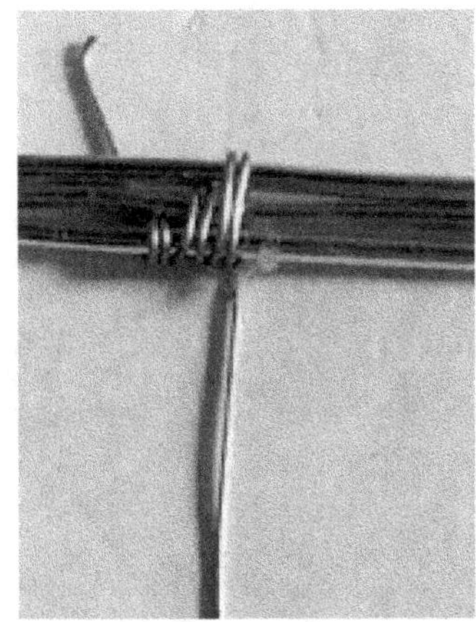

10. Repeat steps #7 and #5, respectively.

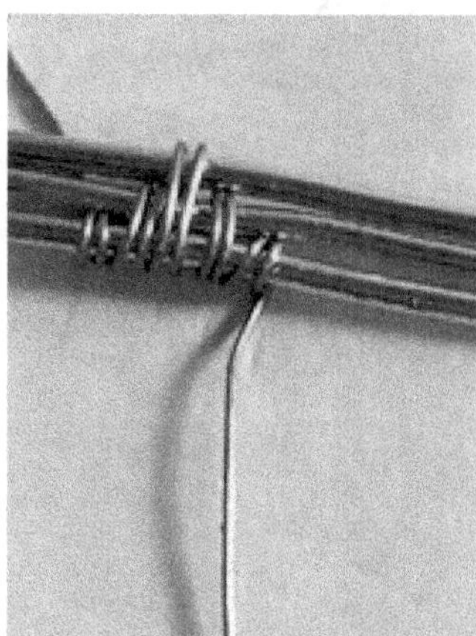

11. Repeat steps #7, #9, #7, and then #5 to continue the pattern until you are close to the end of the base wires. Leave 5 mm (0.2 in) free at the end of the base wires.

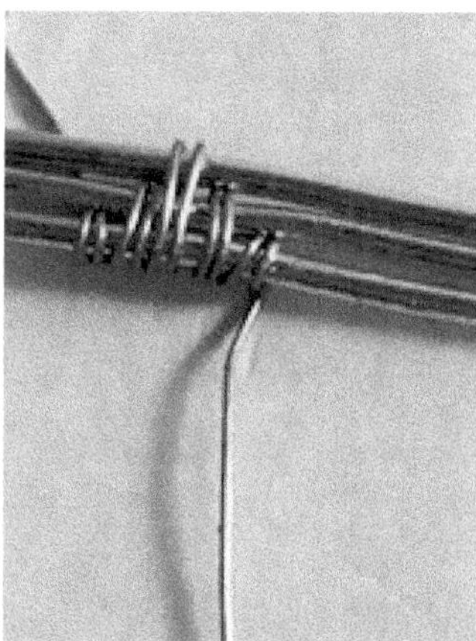

12. Neatly finish off the weaving piece and put it aside for later use.

Figure-8 Stitch

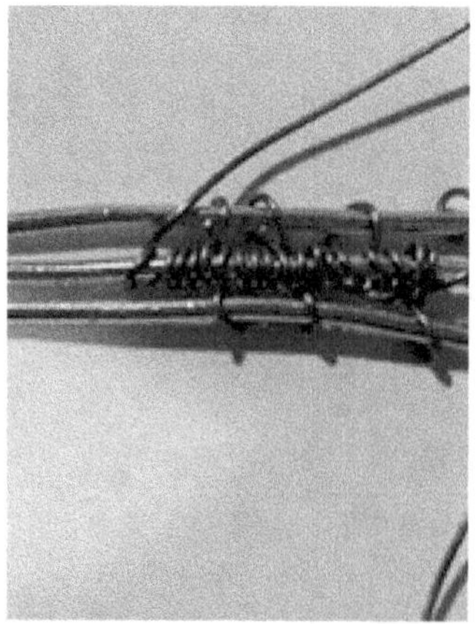

This is the figure-8 stitch. Although it only uses three base wires, it can be a little tricky so take your time with it.

1. Cut three pieces of base wire (BW1, BW2, and BW3).
2. Cut one piece of weaving wire.
3. For this weave, BW1 will be the middle base wire, BW2 will be the top base wire, and BW3 will be the bottom base wire.
4. Holding BW1 horizontally, position the weaving wire vertically at the back of BW1, leaving a small tail at the top. The tail should be long enough to make a small loop when you are done with the pattern to finish off the piece.

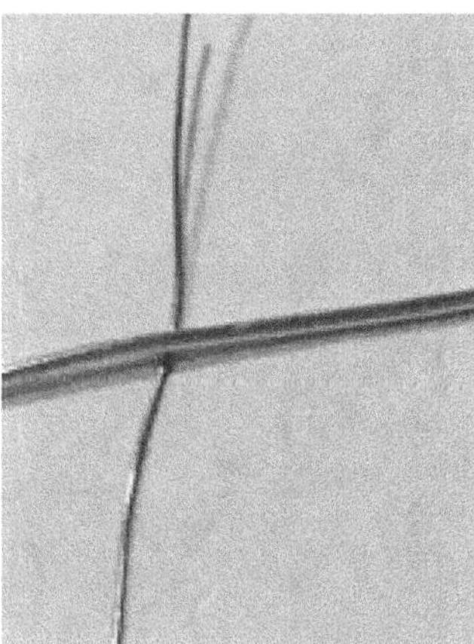

5. Make five loops around BW1 by pulling the weaving wire up around the bottom of BW1 and then over and around the back of BW1. Repeat the loop a second time to make two loops. Position BW2 horizontally on top of BW1.

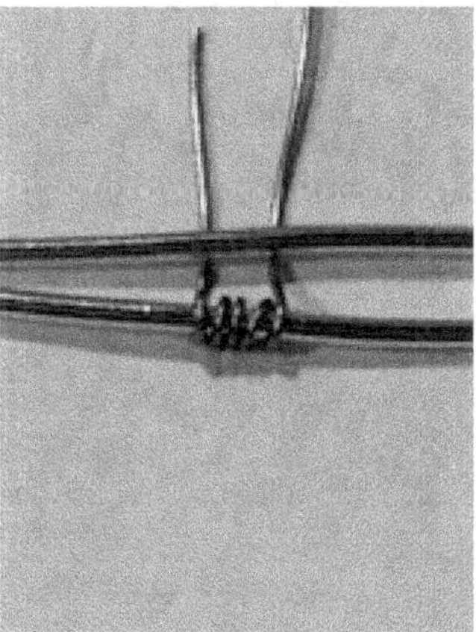

6. Make one loop around BW2 by pulling the weaving wire behind BW2 and then over the top of BW2 through the gap between BW2 and BW1. Pull the weaving wire under BW1.

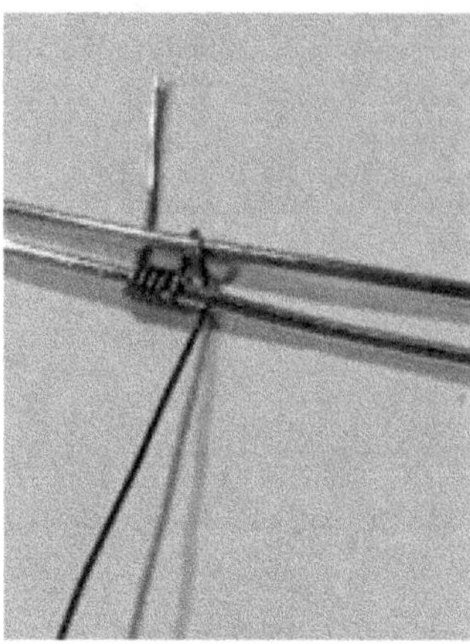

7. Make one loop around BW1 by pulling the weaving wire up around the bottom of BW1 and over the top of BW1 by pushing the wire through the gap between BW1 and BW2.

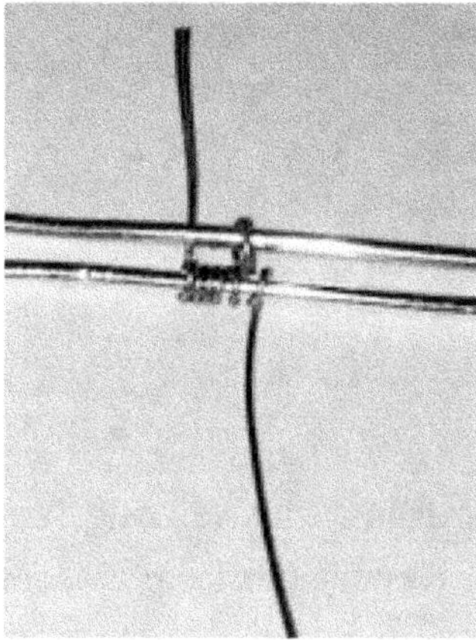

8. Place BW3 below BW1 with the weaving wire positioned behind BW3.

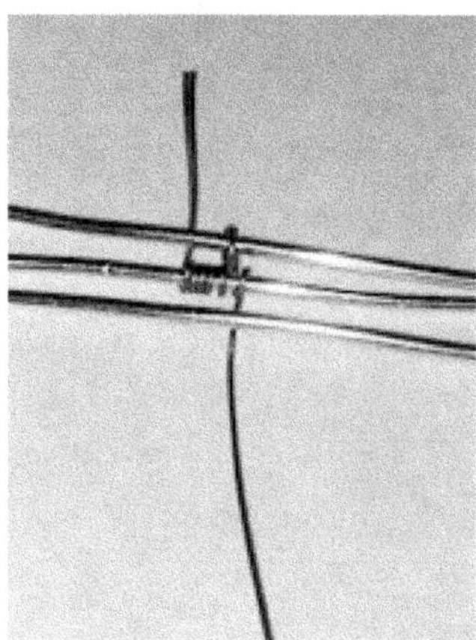

9. Make one loop around BW3 by pulling the weaving wire up and around the bottom of BW3 and then through the gap between BW3 and BW1. Pull the weaving wire up and over BW1.

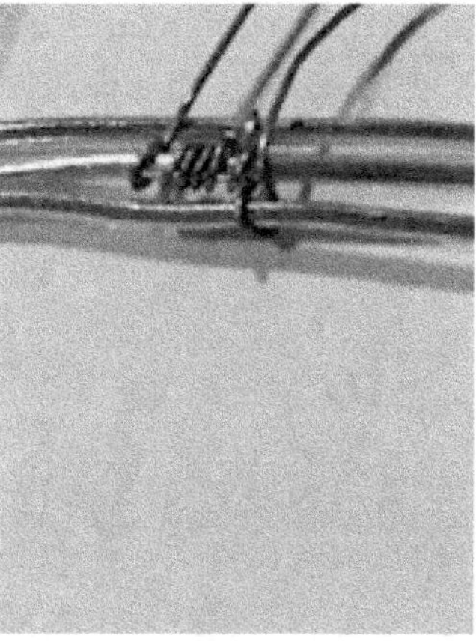

10. Repeat steps #5, #6, #7, and #9, respectively.

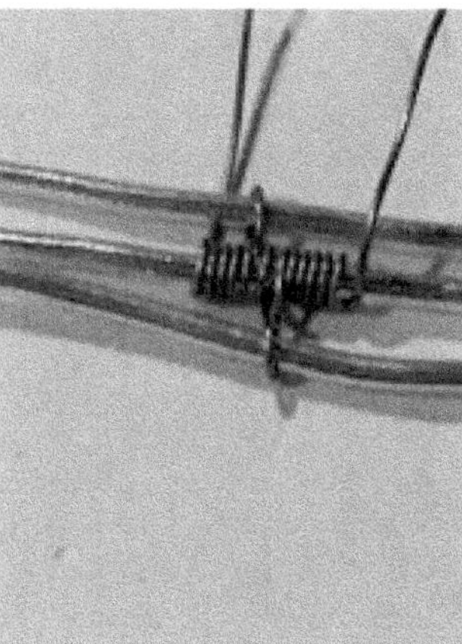

11. Repeat the pattern until you are close to the end of the base wires. Leave 5 mm (0.2 in.) free at the end of the base wires.

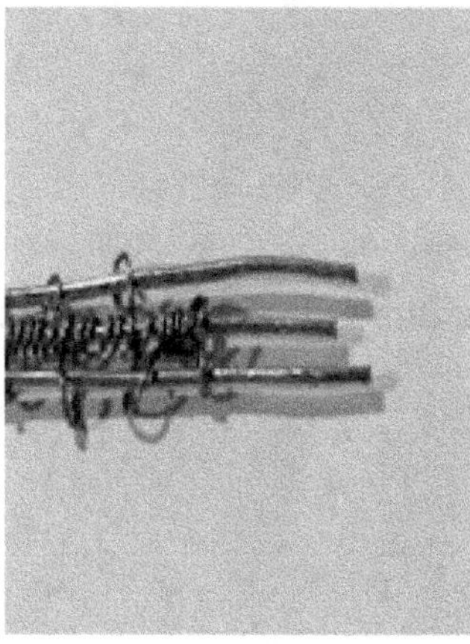

12. Neatly finish off the weaving piece and put it aside for later use.

Finishing Off the Weave

When you start a weave, a tail piece gets left behind. It is necessary so that the weaving wire can be pulled taut to keep the piece from unraveling. However, when you are done weaving, it is no longer needed. The same is true for any weaving wire left over at the end of the weaving piece.

Both ends should be cut off. This is very simple but will require a flush cutter and long nose pliers.

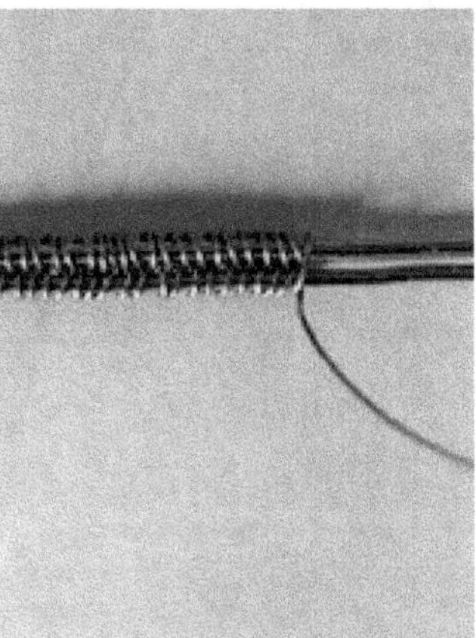

1. Before cutting off the leftover weaving wire, twist it so that it is at the back of the piece.
2. With the flush cutter, cut off both the beginning tailpiece and the leftover weaving wire at the end of the weave. Cut the wire as close to the base wire as possible.

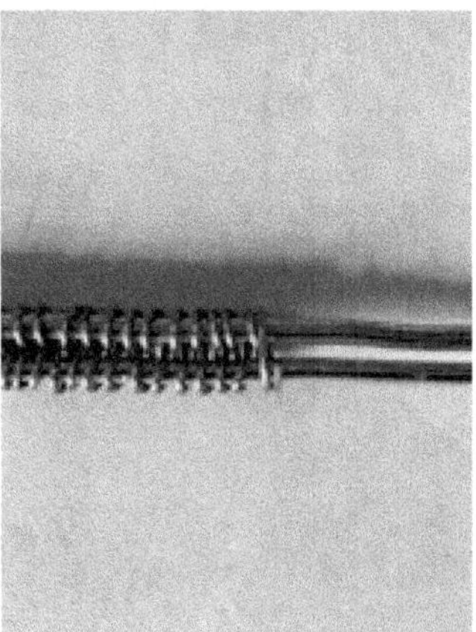

3. With the long-nose pliers, gently squash the sharp edge down so that it stays flush against the base wire. Make sure that it is tight since this will secure your weave. You should also have no sharp edges left.

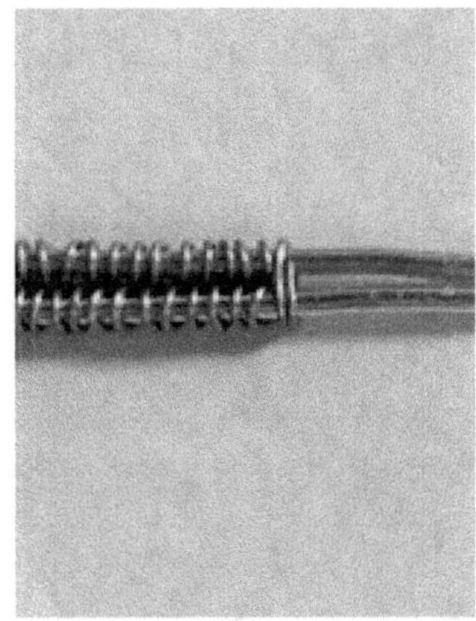

4. Weaving piece should be left with no long wires hanging off it.

CHAPTER 3: TECHNIQUES

There are a few wire jewelry making techniques that can produce interesting designs individually or together. Here are some of the most popular techniques used with wire weaving.

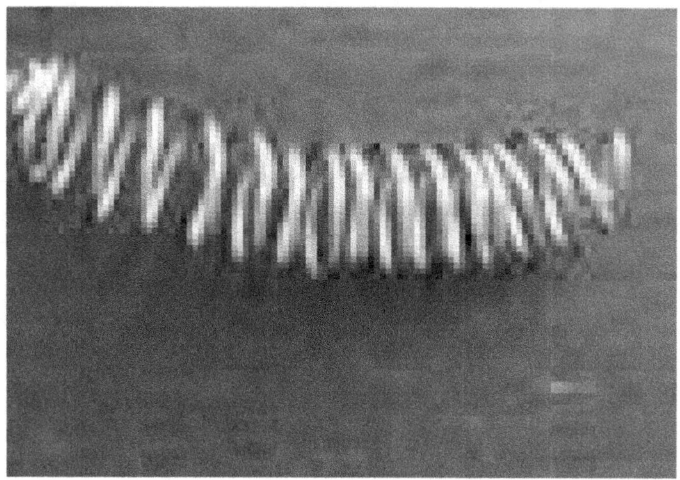

Coiling

Coils are used in many applications. In wire weaving, you can have tight or loose coils and use twisted wire to get some interesting effects. For this technique, the softer wire is wrapped around a hardcore called mandrel. It can be any material as long as it is harder than the coiling wire.

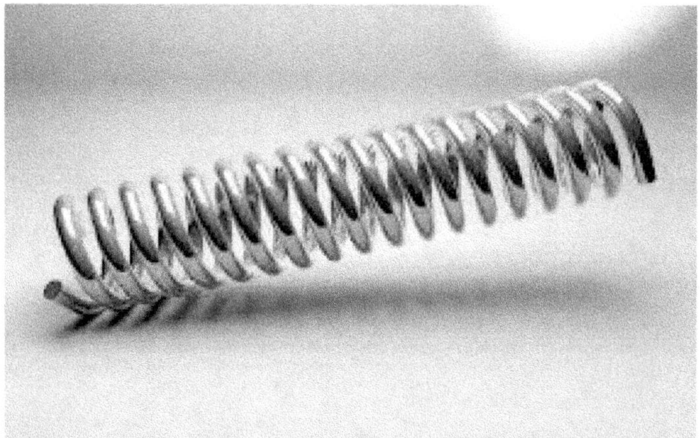

Spiral Coil

The core wire is harder than the wrapping wire because it keeps the coil stable and enables it to bend however it should. If you are using a temporary mandrel just to get the coils, it is best to make it out of strong material. When coiling around the temporary mandrel, leave a little bit of space to be able to easily slip the coil off.

When you slip the coil off of the temporary mandrel, make sure to firmly stabilize the two ends. Otherwise, they will get deformed. Coiling with a wire mandrel in the middle is a lot more stable and easier to bend without disrupting the coils.

This technique is usually used to make jump rings, bracelets, pendants, etc. It lends a unique look to a piece of wire jewelry and can be incorporated into both wrapping and weaving.

The wire used for coiling is any metal that is capable of holding a coil, such as copper, silver, gold, etc.

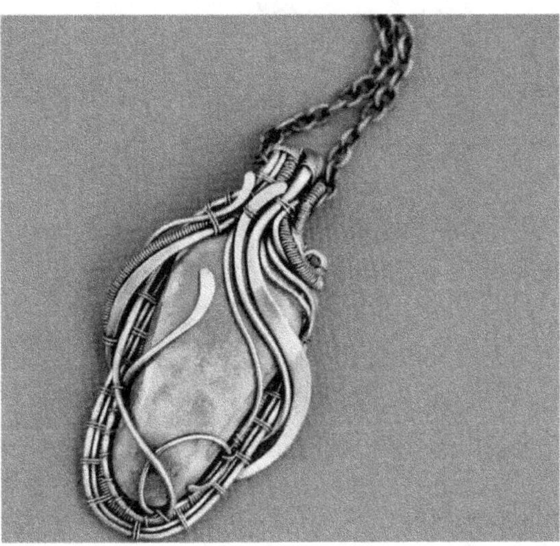

Wrapping

Wrapping is another ancient technique that involves wrapping wires, beads, semi-precious stones, and others to create a design. Instead of intricate weaves, the metal is manipulated through bending, wrapping, and hammering to get the desired effect.

Using jewelry findings and wire, components are made and connected together by bending, twisting, shaping, or other mechanical means. Wire wrapping is done without using solder, glue, or any source of heat to bind or bond substances together.

The wire in this technique is bent into loops, swirls, coils, and other decorative shapes before being wrapped around itself, a bauble of sorts, or findings to finish the piece off. Usually, the loops are linked to other loops or swirls to make more creative jewelry. The metal can be smoothed out by a hammer or mallet. Pliers are also used in helping with the intricate and tough bends, while wire cutters are used to cut the metal.

The wire for wire bending is similar to what you use in coiling and weaving. You can use something like beading wire, copper, memory wire, silver, gold, aluminum, and bronze.

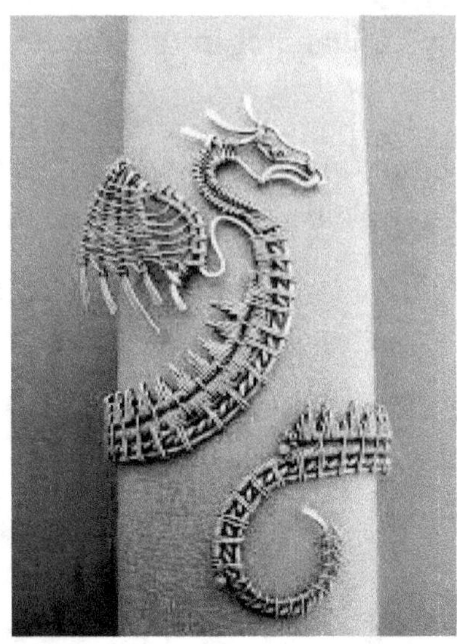

Weaving

Wire weaving involves weaving one wire between two or more base wires. Usually, the base wires are thicker and harder than the weaving wire, which is soft and malleable.

Weaving gives wire jewelry some dimension and lovely textures. It has been around since ancient times and can be applied to the creation of jewelry, ornaments, wire-framed baskets, etc.

When you are weaving, you can incorporate beads, stones, and other jewelry items to create beautiful designs. There are different styles of weaves and patterns that can be combined with both coiling and wrapping techniques.

Like the two mentioned above, weaving is done without the use of various products like glue, heat, or solder. Instead, the weaves are finished off by tightening the wires to ensure that they are bonded naturally together.

The metals used in weaving are the same as the ones used for coiling and wrapping, although the gauges will differ between the base and weaving wires. Copper and craft wires are the most inexpensive options for you.

CHAPTER 4: PROJECT

Follow the pattern below for a simple yet elegant woven bracelet that you can wear or gift to a loved one. It is made from copper. As such, it will complement any outfit or be worn for most occasions.

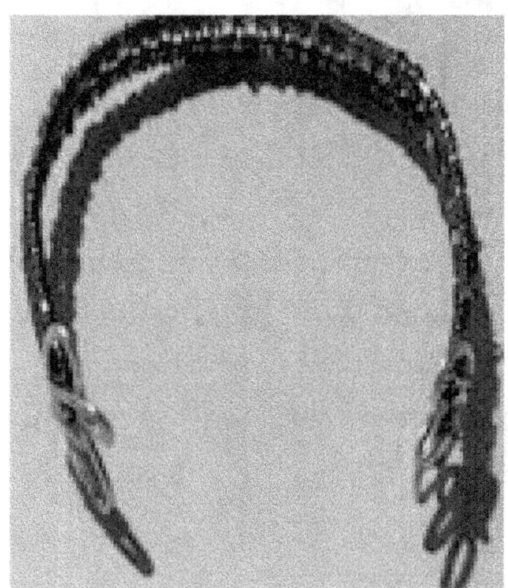

Woven Bracelet

This woven bracelet is a beautiful, classical pattern that is easy to learn and do. It can be made with the elegant straight curve cuff design. You can also give it a bit more character with different bracelet ends.

Similarly, you can make the same bracelet by trying a few weaving stitches that you may have seen in the previous chapter. If you want to get really adventurous, why not experiment with mashing some weave patterns together or experimenting with your own styles?

For this tutorial, though, we are going to stick with the straight cuff design that will require a bit of wire wrapping to finish off the ends.

Items Needed

- 26-gauge copper wire, which will be used for the weaving wire
- Flush cutter for the 26-gauge weaving wire
- 16-gauge copper wire, which will be used for the base wires
- Memory wire shears for cutting the 16-gauge wire
- Chain nose or long nose pliers
- Round nose pliers or some type of mandrel
- Wire straighteners, which are not compulsory but nice to have as the longer base wires can get a little out of shape
- A round tin or something similar to get the shape of the bracelet when you are done weaving
- Protective glasses
- Magnifying glass

Pre-Weaving Reminders

1. Using the memory wire shears, cut four base wires from the 16-gauge copper wire to fit the desired wrist size. Make the base wires a little longer than needed to leave about 20 to 30 mm (0.8 to 1.9 in.) on both sides. It is easier to cut off extra base wires than add on them, so making the base wires a bit longer is a good idea when starting out.
2. Cut one weaving wire from the 26-gauge copper wire. Make it 2.5 times longer than the length of your base wires. Be careful not to have the weaving wire too long, though, as it gets difficult to manipulate. With the weaving wire, it is not that difficult to add on the wire. (See the "Splicing On Additional Wire" section of this tutorial.)
3. For this project, we are going to have four base wires, namely BW1, BW2, BW3, and BW4. BW1 will be the top wire, BW2 will be the second wire, BW3 will be the third wire, and BW4 will be the bottom wire.
4. We will also use a four-loop snake stitch here. This is a lovely stitch for bracelets and necklaces as it is simple yet elegant. Besides, it can enhance the classic lines of this piece.

Creating the Bracelet

1. Start weaving in at about 38.1 mm (1.5 in.) from the edge of the base wires.
2. As there are four lengthy base wires, it may be easier to use a ring clamp to control and secure them. If you do not have one, you can use any clamp with rubber, plastic, or leather jaws, considering it will not damage or nick the metal. This is not compulsory, but it makes holding and manipulating longer base wires a lot easier.
3. Hold BW1 horizontally in your fingers and place the weaving wire vertically at the back of BW1. Leave a tail of about 35 to 40 mm (1.38 to 1.58 in) long, which will be used to finish off the left end of the bracelet once the weave is done.

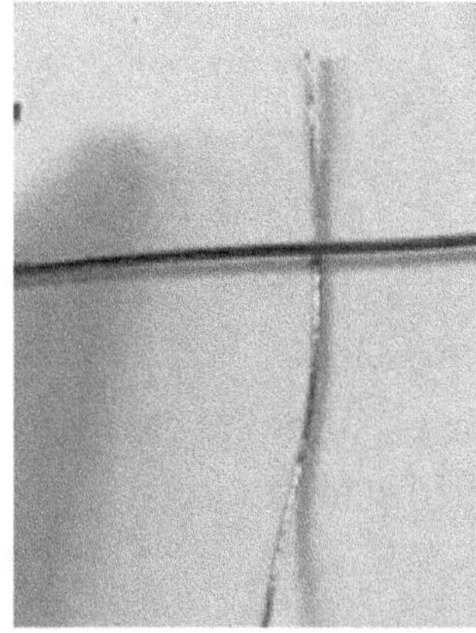

4. Position BW2 below BW1 and make four loops over both BW2 and BW1 with the weaving wire. Make the loops by pulling the weaving wire up and around the bottom of BW2 and then over the top of BW1. Pull the weaving wire down and around the back of BW1 and BW2. Repeat the loop three more times to create four loops.

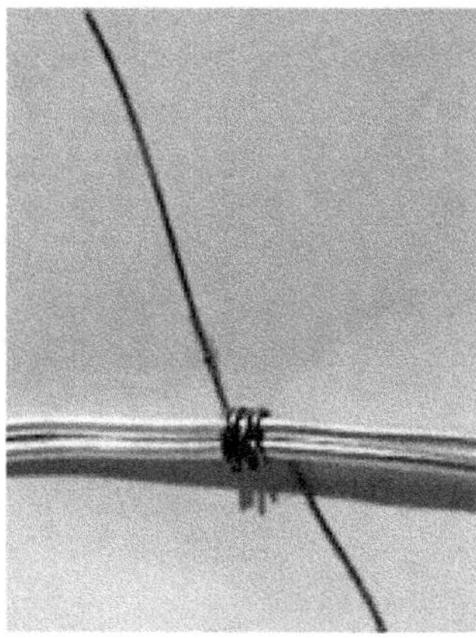

1. Position BW3 below BW2. Position BW4 below BW3. If you are going to use a clamp to secure all four base wires into position, this will be the best time to take it out. BW1 and BW2 should be flush against each other; the same goes for BW3 and BW4. There should be a small gap between BW2 and BW3, though, so that you can still push the weaving wire between them.
2. Make four loops over BW3 and BW4 by pulling the weaving wire up and around the bottom of BW4 and then over the top of BW3. Push the weaving wire between BW2 and BW3 and then pull it down the back of BW3 and BW4. Repeat the same loop three more times. On the last (fourth) loop, pull the weaving wire through the gap in between BW3 and BW2 and then pull weaving wire behind BW2 and BW1.

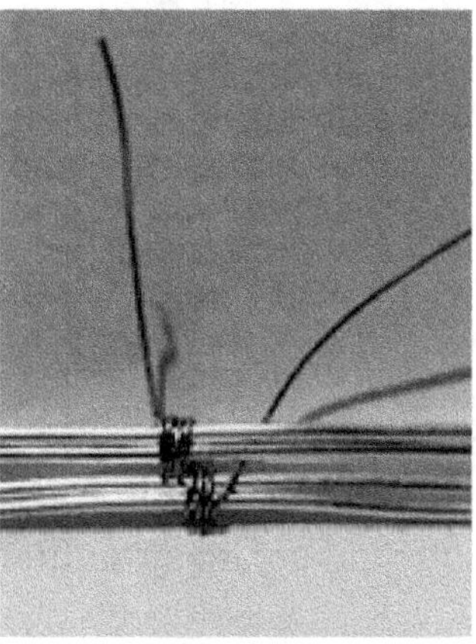

3. Make four loops around BW1 and BW2. On the fourth loop, pull the weaving wire through the gap between BW2 and BW3. Then, pull the weaving wire behind BW3 and BW4.

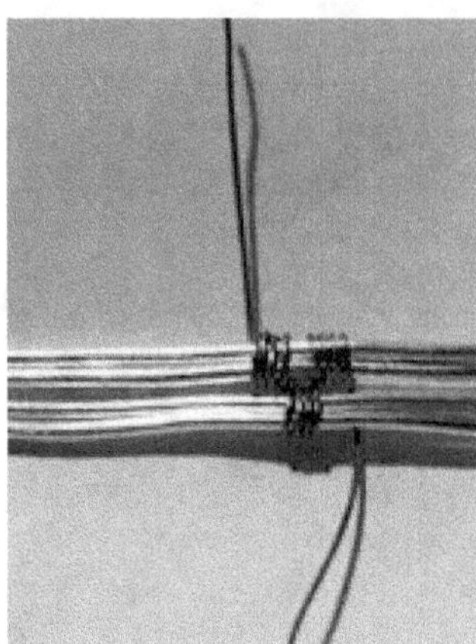

4. Make four loops over BW3 and BW4 like you did in step #6.
5. Repeat steps #7 and #6, respectively.
6. Repeat the pattern until you are close to the end of the base wires. Leave 38.1 mm (1.5 in.) free at the end of the base wires.

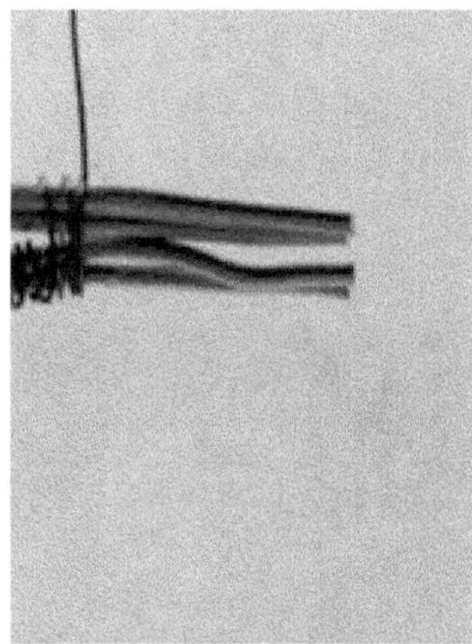

7. You may find getting the loops straight and tight a little tricky. As you pull the weaving wire between two base wires, the loop may end up out of position as well. Well, there is a simple trick to making the weaving wire easier to manipulate and create straighter loops in the correct position.

When you go to create the loop, don't just do so by pushing the weaving in between the intended base wires. First, pull the weaving wire into the loop at the position where you want it to be by creating the start of the loop. Then, steady it by gently placing a fingertip over it. Keeping the loop steady, pull the weaving wire up as if you are going to loop it over. This creates the loop's shape and marks its position. After that, gently bend the weaving wire to pull it through the two base wires and then finish off the loop. Doing so stops the loop from slanting off to the side.

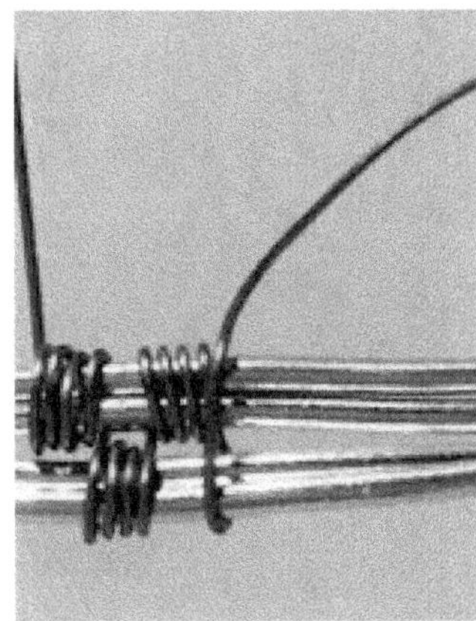

1. Once you have completed the weave, you will need to finish off the two ends of the bracelet and remove the extra pieces of the weaving wire.
2. At the beginning of the bracelet, use the weaving wire tailpiece and make two loops over BW1, BW2, BW3, and BW4. Finish off with the end of the tailpiece at the back of the bracelet. Cut any extra pieces of weaving wire with the flush cutters as close to the base wire as possible.
3. Take the flat nose pliers and squash down the cut edge of the weaving wire. Run your fingers over it to ensure that there are no rough or sharp edges.
4. Repeat steps #13 and #14 for the end piece of the bracelet.

Before Creating the Ending Loop

1. Make sure that both of the end pieces of the four base wires (BW1, BW2, BW3, and BW4) have the same length. If not, use the memory wire shears to sniff the ends off and even them up. Pull any kinks out of the base wire ends with a straightener or your fingers. Don't use any other tool to do this as it may damage the wire.
2. Once the ends of the weaving wire are even, they need to be finished off with a pattern. This is to hold and secure the weave in place as well as give the bracelet its finishing touch. For this project, we are going to create a four-leaf clover type of look.
3. It does not matter which side you start the end piece on. Hold the bracelet firmly and use the round nose pliers to bend the edges. You can also use the flat nose pliers or even a screwdriver if you do not have round nose pliers.

Creating the End Loop

1. Start with BW4. Take the round nose pliers and bend BW4 into the shape of a petal. To do this, bend it outwards and then around. Bend and pull it into position over BW3 and BW4.

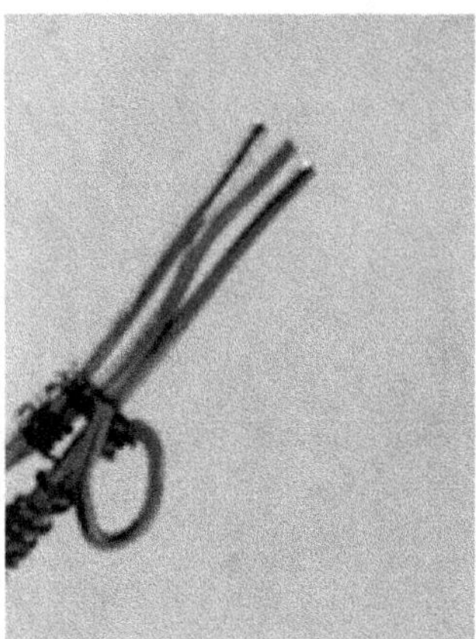

2. Once you have the first petal, use the round nose pliers to bend BW3 around and outwards into a petal. BW3's petal should be positioned on the left side of BW4.
3. Repeat steps #1 and #2 for BW1 and BW2 to finish off the four-leaf clover or get as close to that effect as possible. Remember that this pattern is only an example. You can experiment and create your own design.

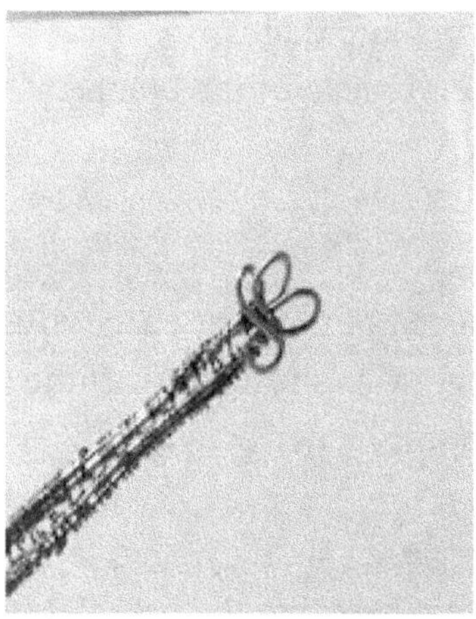

1. Once you are happy with the four-leaf clover, take the flat nose pliers and gently flatten the rough edges of the base wires. Run your fingers over the flower to make sure that there are no sharp points to avoid being cut when wearing the bracelet or handling it.
2. Repeat the same steps above on the other end of the bracelet. Try to mimic the design on the other side well. Alternatively, you can make swirls by twisting BW4, BW3, and BW2 over each other and to the right and then twisting BW1 into a swirl to the left. You can simply curl them forward onto the bracelet in four loops, too. This shows that there are many ways to finish off the bracelet.

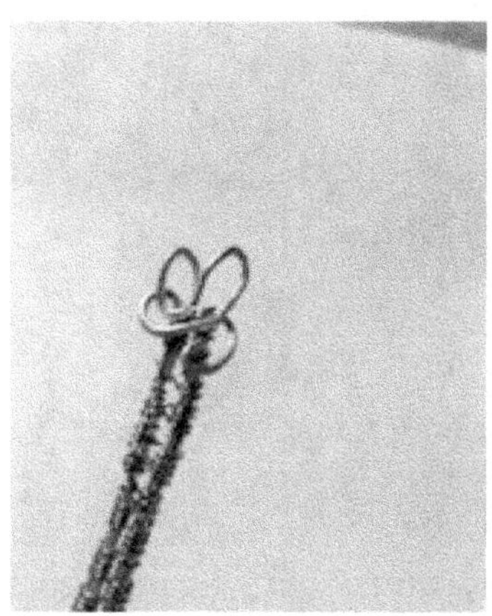

Creating the Bracelet Shape

1. Once both ends of the bracelet are done, you need to turn it into a round bracelet shape. This is usually done with a bracelet mandrel or any circular object that will not break when you apply a little bit of pressure or roll it.
2. To give an example of the different objects that you can use, we are going to use a tin can. It must still be full to be able to hold its shape without buckling when you wrap the bracelet around it.

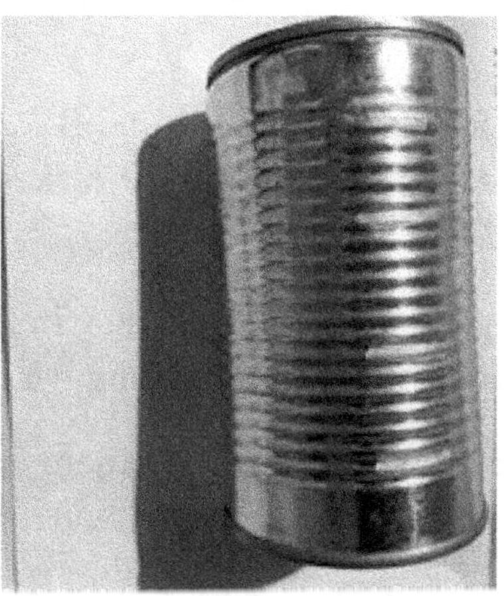

3. Lay the tin on a flat surface, take the bracelet, and lay it over the top of the tin. Gently flatten the bracelet around the tin to give it a rounded shape. Before removing it, you can take the pliers and straighten the base wires if need be.

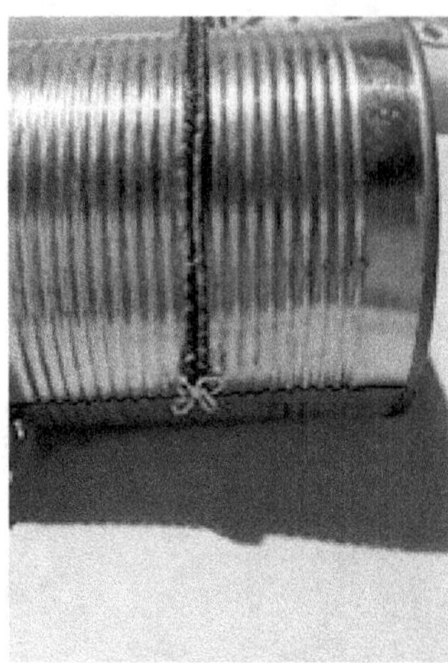

4. Once the bracelet has been shaped on the mandrel, gently lift it off and fit it to your wrist. Bend it into the shape of your wrist to give it its final look.

Tips for Finishing Off the Bracelet

As you weave with the longer base wires, you may find them getting tangled over each other. This is a great weave to try for everyone as it uses pairs to weave the weaving wire over and keeps the pairs flush against each other.

Use a bit of clear tape and wrap it around the end of BW1 and BW2. Do the same for BW3 and BW4. This will stop them from tangling and speed up the process as it makes weaving between the base wires a lot simpler. Plus, it will be a lot less awkward to handle.

If you do not have a ring clamp for the starting end of the base wire, use some tapes around those edges, too. It will also stop the base wires from slipping out of the weaving wire loops.

It is advisable to wear protective glasses while working with the wire because you sit with your face close to the weaving wire. Some weaving wires are really springy and tend to fly all over the place when you are using it. If you get hit, this can do a lot of damage to your eyes. Wire cuttings also serve as a potential hazard to you.

A magnifying glass will help you see where you have gone wrong in your pattern or need to tighten up loose loops. As they are quite small, you cannot always do that with your naked eyes. You can even combine protective glasses with a magnifying glass.

That is it — you have created your first woven piece of jewelry. You can make a thinner bracelet by using two or three bars. Make it thicker by adding bars, get creative with it, and experiment. This simple pattern can be turned into a lot of different designs.

Try to finish the loops in various formations. If you want to get really artsy, try to use a bit of wirework and hammer to manipulate the metal into different shapes.

CHAPTER 5: HELPFUL WIRE WEAVING TIPS

Wire

Wire Shape

The wire shape is what the wire looks like at the cross-section, which is the end where the wire has been cut.

Round Wire

The round wire shape is the most common and widely used wire shape. All the exercises in this tutorial are done using the round wire type.

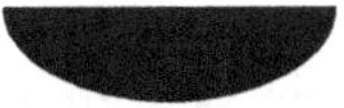

Half-Round Wire

The half-round wire is normally used in conjunction with the square wire. Its flat side is positioned on the square wire to connect a few adjacent pieces made from the square wire. The round side of the half-round wire is left visible so that the joint is not too obvious. This technique is known as banding.

Square Wire

The round wire gives jewelry a smooth, even look, but the design can get a bit monotonous. To put a different aesthetic look on a common design, one should try using square wire. The corners of the wire change the design's appearance. They tend to be a lot better in getting wires flush against each other than round wire. Square wire is great for banding designs and can be used with a pin vise for even more effect.

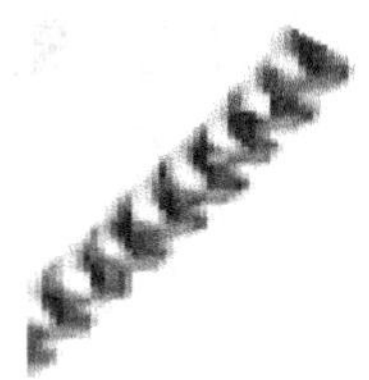

Twisted or Fancy Wire

The twisted or fancy wire is made from coiling either round or square wire. Twisted wires give weaving a more textured look and are all about the aesthetics. You can also buy it pre-made.

Wire Conversion Table

Wire Gauges

The diameter (width) of the wire is called the gauge. It can be abbreviated as "ga." There are two standard gauge systems:

- American Wire Gauge (AWG) system, which is used in the United States and Canada; and
- Standard Wire Gauge (SWG) system, which is sometimes used in the United Kingdom.

Most of Europe and other countries use the metric system and measure in millimeters (mm), although Great Britain and other countries may still use the imperial system and measure in inches (in.).

It is important to note that, when working with wire gauges, the bigger the wire gauge number is, the smaller the wire diameter is. The smaller the gauge number is, the bigger the wire diameter is. For instance, a wire with a gauge of 6 is equivalent to 0.162 inches or 4.11 mm. Meanwhile, a wire with a gauge of 28 is equivalent to 0.008 inches (0.203 mm).

Below is a chart with the most popular wire weaving gauges conveniently converted to inches and millimeters.

AWG Wire Gauge Conversion Chart		
AWG Gauge (ga)	Millimeters (mm)	Inches (in.)
6	4.11	0.162
8	3.27	0.129
9	2.91	0.114
10	2.56	0.102
12	2.05	0.081
14	1.63	0.064

15	1.45	0.057
16	1.30	0.051
17	1.14	0.045
18	1.02	0.040
19	0.914	0.036
20	0.813	0.032
21	0.737	0.029
22	0.635	0.025
24	0.508	0.020
25	0.455	0.018
26	0.406	0.016
28	0.320	0.013
30	0.254	0.010
32	0203	0.008

How to Gauge Wire

Wire gauging, as explained above, works in opposition to the wire gauge number. For instance, if the wire gauge number is 6, the wire will be thicker than a wire with a gauge of 15, and so on.

The reason why it was designed this way is that the wire sizes were historically measured by a draw plate. A draw plate is a die-cast plate usually made of steel and used to thin wires with. The steel passes through the holes in the drawplate while the gauge is measured by how many times the wire has to go through the drawplate before being measured. The fewer times it passes through means that it is a thicker wire; the more times it passes through means that it is a thinner wire.

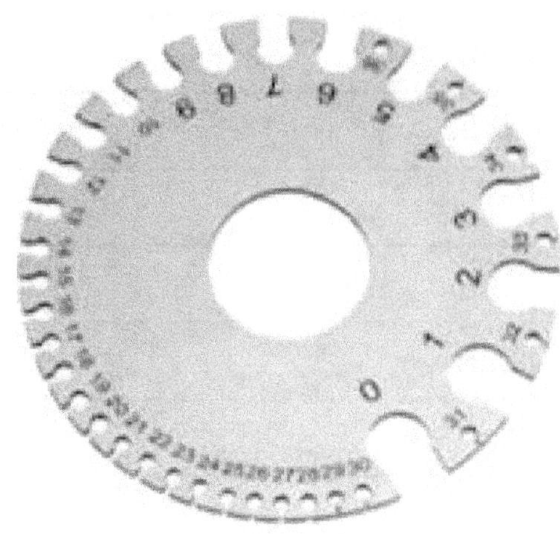

Wire Gauging Tool

The best way to gauge wire is by using a wire gauging tool. The easy ones come as a metal wheel with slots grooved into the sides of the wheel. On the one side, they will have the gauge size number beneath each groove. On the other side, they will either be in millimeters or inches, depending on if the manufacturer uses the metric or imperial system.

There are many types of wire gauging tools that come in a straight ruler or a fan format, which has moving arms with different gauge sizes. No matter what style you use, though, they all work in the same way. Furthermore, wire gauging tools usually come in a nice protective sleeve for easy storage and protection. It is a good idea to store your gauging tool in its case to ensure that it lasts longer.

To use the wire gauge, hold it comfortably in your hand or grip it securely in a vice of some sort. Take the wire that needs to be gauged and slip it through one of the openings that best represents its size. The wire should easily slide into the opening; it should not be too tight or too loose. The wire should fit almost perfectly through the opening to know the wire gauge well.

Choosing the Best Gauge for Your Project

Although this is not an exact science, here is a guide as to what gauge wire to use for bracelets, neck collars, ornaments, and various other weaving projects.

- **10 gauge** wire comes in a dead-soft temper, which means that it will require some extra tools for bending and cutting of the metal. It needs sturdier jewelry-making tools than those used for thinner wires. It can be used to make neck collars, thick bangles, cuff bracelets, and even some woven ornaments.
- **12 gauge** wire is also usually available in a dead-soft temper and used for the same applications as the 10 gauge. E.g., rings, neck collars, cuff bracelets, frames, etc. This gauge wire will require the same heavy-duty jewelry tools for manipulating, weaving, and cutting.
- **14 gauge** wire normally comes in a dead-soft temper and can be difficult to bend, depending on what metal it is made out of. This gauge is used to create things like rings, cuff bracelets, and even rivets. It is excellent for making clasps, frames (structure wire), jump rings, and mixed media projects as

well. Like the other two wires, it will require heavy-duty jewelry tools.

- **16 gauge** wire comes in either half-hard or dead-soft temper and will require heavy-duty jewelry tools to manipulate and cut. It is a good wire to make chainmaille jewelry, jump rings, clasps, frames, rings, cuff bracelets, neck collars, and bangles.
- **18 gauge** wire is a lot easier to manipulate by hand and can be used in conjunction with normal or regular cutting and shaping tools. It is a good wire for creating most handmade items, as well as rings, neck collars, bracelets, and chainmaille jewelry. It is also used to make delicate clasps, jump rings, bails, and frames.
- **20 gauge** wire can be easily shaped by hand and regular jewelry making tools. It is good for creating delicate earring loops and other handcrafted findings. It can be used to make things like ear wires, frames, spirals, headpins, eye pins, hoop earrings, and wire settings that can take medium-sized stones. It is also great for making bails for light stones, intricate clasps, jump rings, split rings, and open-link chains.
- **21 and 22 gauge** wires can be shaped by hand and only requires the use of standard jewelry tools. It is great for making ear wires, frames, spirals, small clasps, small to medium stone settings, jump rings, headpins, eye pins, wire wrapped links, and open-link chains.
- **24 gauge** wire is something that weavers buy a lot due to its versatility. It is also easy to manipulate by hand and only requires standard jewelry tools to work with. Although it can be used as a frame for smaller wire pieces, it is more recommended as a support frame. This gauge is excellent for coiling, binding, weaving, setting smaller stones, as well as making spirals, small jump rings, and headpins.
- **26 gauge** wire is in between being a fine wire and something with a bit of backbone strength. It is usually used for coiling, making balled headpins, weaving, and wire wrapping for briolettes and some smaller beads or stones.
- **28 and 30 gauge** wires are more for weaving or wrapping around other stronger wires. They are not recommended as a structural wire or for creating open-loop links as they are too fine. They need to be used with fine-tipped jewelry tools for cutting and shaping. These wires are really, really tiny and very easy to manipulate by hand. They are also very breakable and can become kinked if not handled properly. They are mainly used for weaving, coiling, and wrapping, although they cannot hold beads or other findings well.

Wire Temper (Hardness)

When you work with wire, you hear about gauges, as well as the tempers or hardness of the metal. The latter can affect what you can make with the wire. For instance, for the frames, you want a wire that does not easily bend. For the weave, you need a wire that can be easily manipulated into a pattern for your jewelry piece.

A wire's hardness is measured by how easy it bends or resists bending. In wire weaving, this plays an important role in choosing wire for the frame and weaving around the frame.

Another important factor to keep in mind when measuring the hardness of a metal is its type. Some metals may have the same gauge but are a bit softer or harder than other types of metal. Dead-soft gold and silver will not be the same to work with in terms of how they are manipulated into shape as well.

Some wires do not come in different levels of hardness and are just either soft, half-hard, etc. Wires like aluminum only come as a soft wire, for example.

When it comes to jewelry wire, there are three different levels of hardness:

- **Dead-soft** or **soft** wire is quite difficult to work with as it offers little or no resistance when you bend it. Although it may seem like a good thing when you are weaving or wrapping wire, it makes it challenging to form tight angles. The wire also tends not to hold a shape too well and is not usually recommended to use as a frame or base structure. However, it seems great for coiling things around.
- **Full-hard** wire resists bending. The good thing about that is that it retains its shape. The bad thing is that it is prone to breaking due to brittleness. Thus, you cannot use this metal for forging, coiling, or even shaping.
- **Half-hard** wire is the metal in between dead soft and full hard. It is soft enough to manipulate into the shape that you want but hard enough to retain its shape. It is also good for making tight bends, coiling, wrapping, weaving, and creating structural frames, depending on the wire gauge.

Work hardening is not a wire hardness but is a technique used to make softer metal a bit harder. This is done in a few ways, such as hammering against an anvil with a hammer or mallet. It can also involve twisting the wire or pulling it through a drawplate repeatedly.

Wire wrapping itself can be used to harden wire, as well as coiling. Some softer metal needs to be work-hardened to ensure that they can maintain their shape.

Wire Metals

The most widely used metal for wire weaving is **copper**. It is a lot more affordable than precious metal, holds its shape well, and can still be oxidized to give it an heirloom effect. **Silver** is another metal that is quite easy to work with but is quite pricey. There are different categories of silver for wire weavers. Using a precious metal, it may be a good idea to try a silver-filled wire type.

There are a few different categories of wire that you can get for wire weaving.

Base Metals

- **Aluminum** is a great metal to use when starting out with wire weaving as it is quite easy to bend and sculpt with. It also comes in an array of colors to make nice, bright pieces.
- **Artistic** wire is very soft and comes in a multitude of bright and even luminous colors to add that bit of sparkle to wire weaving. It is completely malleable as it has a copper core with a color coating that comes in 10 to 30 gauge wire sizes.

There is also the silver-plated artistic wire that has a high shine and can be bare or tinned. The bare artistic wire naturally patina with age to give a truly great heirloom effect on jewelry pieces, to be specific. Most of these are enamel-coated so their color does not strip.

- **Brass** has a bright golden color that gives jewelry pieces a warm rich texture. It is a very versatile metal, although it is a bit stiffer than other metals, thus making it just a bit harder to work with.

Because brass is a little less forgiving than other wires, it is prone to getting kinks and knots if not handled correctly. This wire is more for an intermediate to experienced wire weaver because of that.

- **Bronze** is similar to copper in texture, but it is a bit stiffer than that, so it is a bit harder to work with. This hard metal does not require work hardening, but it is not recommended for beginners. Rather, bronze is more for advanced wire weavers who know how to manipulate hard metals.
- **Copper** is the most common metal used for wire weaving. It is a warm, affordable, and naturally soft metal. It is also not too hard to work harden if need be. You can get both plated and raw copper wires. It comes in gauges of 10 right through to 30 and can be used for most jewelry and ornamental wire weaving projects.

Another reason why copper is so popular is that it has a lovely shine and can be oxidized to create a more antique look. Plus, it is really easy to work with, clean, and polish. It is the best wire for beginners to start practicing with.

- Gold-plated wire usually has a copper base coated with a very thin layer of real gold. They are usually not the best wire to use for weaving as their coatings tend to be too fragile for the application.

- **Nickel silver (German silver)** wire is a mix of zinc, nickel, and copper. It does not actually have silver in it. Even though nickel silver is a good alternative to the said metal due to its affordability, a lot of people are allergic to it. This wire is also harder than copper and, therefore, more challenging to work with. It is on par with bronze in terms of hardness and is better suited for intermediate or advanced weavers.
- **Silver-plated** wire typically has a copper base coated with a very thin layer of silver. Like the gold-plated material, it is not suitable for wire weaving applications as their coatings are very fragile.

Precious Metals

- **Argentium Sterling Silver** is a precious metal with a high silver content of silver. It seldom tarnishes and is a bit stronger than fine silver but is not as pliable or springy. It comes in 93.5% or 96% silver gradings. Argentium sterling silver is an easy metal to heat or work harden and is as malleable as sterling silver is. If you are making precious metal wire jewelry, this may be an excellent metal to try.
- **Karat gold** is a precious metal jewelry wire that is really expensive and comes in round wires of 10, 14, 18, 22, and 24 karat gold. It is usually only used by experienced jewelers.
- **0.999 fine silver wire** is pure silver as it contains 99.9% silver (hence the name). Some like working with it since the material is as smooth and soft as real butter. Fine silver is very expensive. It is naturally tarnishing resistant and also falls under the category of half-hard metal, which is one of the most perfect metals for wire weaving. If you weave with fine silver, you should use it as the core or structure wire with sterling silver.
- **Gold-filled or gold overlay** has a base metal such as copper that is overlaid with a thick layer of gold. Although it is only an overlay, it still falls under the precious metal category as it contains enough gold to make it so. If you want to make gold jewelry, this may be a less expensive alternative to karat gold wire.
- **Silver-filled or silver overlay** has a base metal such as copper that is overlaid with a thick layer of

the precious metal silver. It is also a cheaper alternative for making beautiful silver pieces.

- **0.925 sterling silver** contains 92.5% pure silver and is commonly known as 925 silver. The remaining 7.5% is usually made up of copper. This mix makes it easier to work with and allows the metal to tarnish naturally with age. The wire comes in different gauges and is quite as easy to work with like copper. Although silver is an easy metal to work with, it is more suitable for advanced wire weavers due to its cost.

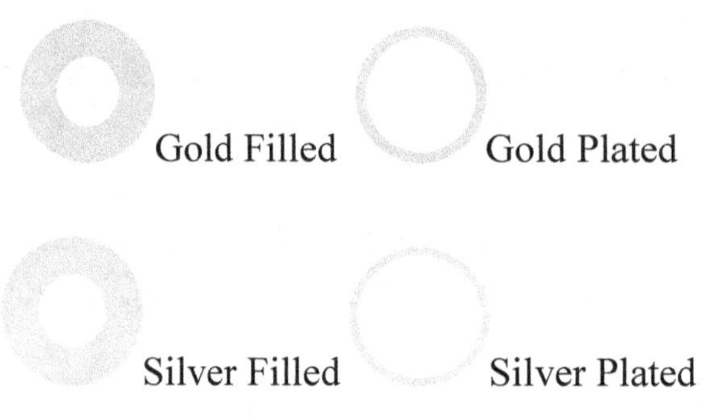

Steel Wire

- **Memory wire** is mainly used in beading and contains a bit of stainless steel. This makes it quite a hard metal, which is why you need memory wire cutters to cut it. Weavers do not usually use this material as it is too springy and likes to hold its coil.
- **Stainless steel** is a full hard metal that can be a bit unforgiving and challenging to work with, especially for beginners. It also takes special wire cutters to cut the metal and is recommended for intermediate to advanced weavers.

Splicing on Additional Wire

To add on an extra run of wire, do not cut it off until you are making a weave around a single base wire. As you pull the wire through and up, trim it with your wire cutters as close to the base wire as possible. Then, take your flat nose pliers and flatten it, running your finger over the area to make sure that it is smooth. Pull the new pieces of wire through with the small tailpiece to the back and behind the base bars. Continue on the pattern from where the wire was cut, and make more loops before cutting the tail off. When you do so, cut it as close to the base wire as possible and do not forget to flatten it with pliers.

LOS, Polishing, and Waxing

Once your jewelry piece is done, you may want to clean or keep it clean for that matter, After all, accessories can become tarnished and dull over time. Here are a few things that you can try.

Liver Of Silver (LOS)

As an oxidation agent, LOS can only be used on metal that has not been treated with an anti-tarnish solution. When used on metals such as silver, gold or copper, the potassium sulfur gives it an aged look or greenish or brownish sheen that is known as a patina effect. It can turn an ordinary piece into something that resembles a family heirloom.

Polishing

There are a few methods that can be used to polish wire jewelry, as well as homemade and shop-bought substances to help with this task. Before buying any product, check the label to find out if it is suitable for your wire or metal. If in doubt, ask for help.

Standard Solutions:

- Brasso
- Nevr Dull polish
- Speed Brite
- Tarn-X-Brass

Home Solutions:

- Lemon juice is for cleaning brass or copper. You can add a few teaspoons of vinegar and baking soda to the lemon juice to create a paste. It will feel a little bit gritty, but that is normal. Use a soft cloth to scrub the paste over the brass or copper. Then, rinse the item with lukewarm water and dry it off with a clean soft, non-fluff cloth.
- White toothpaste is a bit abrasive but gentle as well.
- Dremel polishing tool spins on a wheel and uses different pads for different types of metal. The jewelry is held against the pad as the wheel spins and polishes it.

Waxing

There are different waxes like Micro-crystalline wax that are polished onto jewelry to make it extra shiny. Most jewelry waxes also coat the item with a protective layer to keep it shining and prevent it from tarnishing.

It is important to note that these are only suggestions and do not work on all wire or metal types. Before dipping your entire jewelry in any of the solutions above, you should test the method with a piece of the wire first. It is also not recommended to most of the said polishing or cleaning methods on baubles or stones. For precious metals, check the labels of any solution as most products for brass or copper do not normally work well with gold or silver.

Using Beads, Crystals, and Semi-Precious Stones

You can use all sorts of beautiful beads, crystals, and semi-precious stones with your woven jewelry pieces. Only, you must ensure that the wire is strong enough to support the stone or bauble.

There are a few ways to support a bauble in the weave:

- **Use Wire wrapping technique** where you firmly wrap coils, loops, or bends the weave to firmly hold the stone in place;
- **Use a mid-wire** through the bauble which attaches each side of the piece to hold it firmly in place; or

- **Add a handmade bail** where you add extra beads, as well as a fancy clasp to make the jewelry more detailed.

Pliers

Pliers are an essential tool for jewelry making as they help to twist, flatten, and straighten the wire. There are different shapes and sizes of pliers used on different wire gauges, designs, etc. They come in convenient packs with sets of four to six, too, which may be a good buy for beginners.

Bent Nose Pliers

The nose on these pliers taper down and look like claws. They are ideal for getting in between the wire or other hard-to-reach places. They are also a bit better at opening and closing jump rings than normal straight nose pliers.

Chain Nose Pliers

These pliers' noses are flat on the inside but rounded on the outside. They are good for making tight loops, manipulating tight corners, and crimping bead and jump rings.

Flat Nose Pliers

Flat nose pliers have a wide square jaw that tapers to the point and is flat on both sides. They are used for any application that requires a sturdy grip. They are also good at straightening out the wire and flattening the ends.

Flat & Round Nose Pliers

These strange-looking pliers have one end that is flat like the flat-nose pliers and another end that is round like the round nose pliers. On the flat side, there are grooves inside the jaw. These pliers are great for making loops.

Nylon Jaw Pliers

These pliers have fat nylon jaws and are ideal for working with gold and silver or any metal. After all, they do not scratch, scuff, or damage the metal when gripping it. The nylon jaw can also straighten out kinks without damaging the wire.

Round Nose Pliers

As the name suggests, the nose of such pliers is round and tapers to a point at the end. They are used for making various loops in the wire or as a mandrel. They can be quite hard on precious metal and are inclined to leave kinks so care must be taken when using them on silver or gold.

Wire Straighteners

When working with long lengths of wire, you can end up getting knots or kinks. Wire straighteners help to keep the wire straight, especially when you have just released it from the spool, and it springs all over the place.

Cutters

Cutters are a much-needed tool to have in a jewelry making kit. They make it easy to cut wire to the desired length and finish a jewelry piece neatly as they can get in close to the frame. They can also give a wire a much smoother finish so that there are no unsightly jagged edges on it.

End Wire Cutters

Sometimes referred to as nippers, these cutters have a strange-looking square jaw that looks like pinchers. They are used for cutting the harder gauges of wire from 6 to 18. They are great for cutting when using soft metals as their polished heads protect them from damage. The cutter is at the end of the jaw and flat, thus giving a normal cut that is not particularly flush.

Flush Cutters

Flush cutters are the most versatile type of cutters. They come in different sizes to suit the wire or metal being used in the design. They create a smooth cut for an unbroken look that has no rough edges. The one side will be flush, while the other will have a slight point to it.

These cutters can cut soft, hard, and beading wires. Their jaw is angled to the side and called a diagonal jaw shape. They are used where you are going to see the ends of the jewelry and you need the ends to look smooth and professional.

Glass Cutters

They have round disc heads and are capable of cutting the glass or ceramic at an angle, trimming edges, and straightening cuts or circles.

Memory Wire Shears

Such shears are excellent for cutting stainless steel memory wire or other hardwire types. There is a rounded jaw on the side of the cutter that makes a straight cut. If you are using memory wire, you should get this tool as it can ruin the blade on other cutters.

Semi-Flush Cutters

The semi-flush cutters have a wider flush or peak angle when they are cut. They do not give a smooth or finished look, but they still leave the wires without burs. Most jewelry makers use them for splicing on extra wire or where you are able to hide the ends of the wire. The semi-flush cutters are the best cutters for cutting memory wire.

Side Cutters

These wire cutters do not do well on stainless steel and are more suitable for craft wires. As they have a regular jaw shape, they do not give a flush cut.

Stringing Wire Nippers

These cutters are handy if you need to cut soft wire such as copper or steel-reinforced thread wire such as Acculon. Their jaw is angled to the side, and they offer a flush cut.

There are quite a few different pliers and cutter types. The more advanced you get, the better you will understand their uses.

Other Useful Wire Weaving Tools

Anvil

An anvil is a handy tool to have when you are trying to hammer metal. Most jewelry making anvils have a flat end and horn end, but you can also get one with two horn ends. The horn end can work as a sort of mandrel and makes it easy to pummel round metals.

An anvil is also super handy for polishing your pieces.

Bench Block

Bench blocks come in steel and rubbers. The steel ones help get kinks and knots and hardening and burnishing metal. The rubber bench blocks can smoothen the metal without damaging it.

Draw Plates

Draw plates come in varying shapes, sizes, and materials, such as wood and metal. They are great for condensing a wire's diameter without ruining it.

Files and Sandpaper

There are different types of files and sandpaper grits that you can get to smoothen the surface of your pieces. Using them ensures that there are no rough edges or burs. They can also harden the jewelry and remove scratch marks.

A jewelry rock tumbler is a great device to polish, smooth, and clean your jewelry.

Hammers and Mallets

A **ball-peen hammer** has one round, flat side that is usually made of brass. The other side of it is shaped like a ball or rounded conical. They are quite heavy hammers and used for tough wire or metalwork.

A **chasing hammer** has a flat side that's used for striking the materials. Its other side is smaller and used for making patterns or rivets.

A **mallet** is usually made out of rubber or rawhide. You can use it for shaping softer metal without causing too much damage to it.

Magnifying Glasses

Magnifying glasses are really handy for seeing intricate weaves or just helping to get the perfect weave. They come in all shapes and sizes and can be worn as Opti-visors or placed on a moveable stand for ease of use.

Mandrels

Mandrels are used for creating loops, swirls, rings, and spirals.

Ring Weaver

A ring weaver is a handy little jig for making rings, spirals, etc. It can also do a few sizes as the jig pins can move. It is helpful for beginners who want to perfect their stitches without having to handle the base wires on their own.

Wire Clamp

It is quite good to have as well, especially for a beginner. A wire clamp can secure base wires and practice the weaves. It can also help you straighten out kinked, knotted, or twisted wire.

Helpful Links for More Wire Weaving Ideas

Introduction to Wire Weaving Tutorial by Beaducation.com

https://www.youtube.com/watch?v=8cS_z_tem-I

Beaducation has a great wire weaving tutorial for beginners and links to all the tools and materials required to do the tutorial. This particular video shows you how to work the wire and what to watch out for while doing it.

Basic Wire Weaving Tutorial by Rachel at Wire Guild

https://www.youtube.com/watch?v=ad5xamBVEng

This is a very basic video but has a lot of useful information for a new weaver. There are links to other tutorials in Rachel's series as well.

Wire Weaving Tutorial and Tips by Lori Dupuis

https://www.youtube.com/watch?v=kZpJ38TE0F8&list=PLVrx80YTmdVcvHlQ-fd_zsfM6OpLgUnLi

There are tutorials here for beginners and seasoned wire weavers. The series touches on making stitches, adding wire, fixing tensions, as well as other handy tips and tricks.

Snake Wire Weave — Wire Weaving Series by CSL Designs

https://www.youtube.com/watch?v=Anpm1pHuGXA

This is a great series to follow on YouTube. It shows the snake weave, as well as links to even more helpful tutorials in this series. There are also more advanced ones to take you a step further in your weaving game.

CONCLUSION

There is an endless array of ideas, patterns, and styles of jewelry to be made once you have mastered the basics of wire weaving. It does not stop at making wearable items alone. In truth, there is so much more you can do with the craft. E.g., woven ornaments, useful jewelry tree holders, mini woven baskets, bookends, tie clips, and so on.

You are only limited by your imagination when it comes to what you can do with wire weaving. As you gain more experience, you can start to experiment with mixing different stitches to make exciting new patterns. You may even take your art one step further and mix it with wire wrapping. The latter is very closely related to wire weaving only where you used intricate weaves to hold wire and baubles in place wire wrapping uses folds.

With the many different types, colors, and shapes of wire available on the market today, you can make colorful wire weaves to add a bit of flair to your pieces. Once you are comfortable with your abilities, you can branch out and use more expensive metals like silver and gold. Alternatively, there are the gold- and silver-plated wires that work well if you do not want to spend quite as much on the real thing.

Whichever metal you choose to work with, the most important thing is to have fun and enjoy your craft. Get creative, design, and remember that there are no mistakes when it comes to making unique wire weaving pieces! Soon, you will be inspiring others with your outstanding work and making stylish gifts for a bride-to-be, a newborn, or even a prom date. There is nothing like the feeling of seeing someone wearing one of your creations on a special day or every other day for that matter.

If you followed the projects in this tutorial, you should have already made your first pieces of wire jewelry and learned the basic skills. Feel free to go back to the previous chapter to see a few helpful links to some sites that offer more wire weaving techniques and patterns to take your new-found craft even further.

BIBLIOGRAPHY

Locker Group. (2018, May 21). The History of Wire Weaving and Wire Working. Retrieved from https://www.lockergroup.com/history/history-of-wire-weaving/

Rings & Things. (n.d.). Wire Jewelry 101. Retrieved from https://www.rings-things.com/Learn/Wire-Jewelry/#metals

Stice, C. (2016, February 09). What Jewelry Wire Gauge & Hardness do You Need? Retrieved from https://www.halsteadbead.com/articles/jewelers-guide-gauges-tempers

Wendi. (2019, May 11). Jewelry Wire: Everything You Need to Know to Make the Best Choices. Retrieved from https://door44studios.com/jewelry-wire-everything-you-need-to-know-to-make-the-best-choice/

INTERMEDIATE WIRE WEAVING

How to Create Wire Jewelry Without Splurging on Expensive Metals

INTRODUCTION

There's nothing that satisfies the creativity bug quite like making handcrafted, tangible, beautiful items. Artistic outlets come in all shapes and sizes, but some offer more rewarding end results than others. Wire weaving is one such outlet.

Wire weaving is a jewelry-making technique that is used to create both charmingly simple and stunningly complex designs, and if you're reading this, then you've clearly fallen in love with the craft. As one of the oldest techniques for making jewelry still practiced to this day, there's a lot of information out there regarding which weaves to use, what projects to make, and the many variations of materials you can utilize in order to come up with your own unique pieces. It almost becomes overwhelming to sort it all out, especially once you're past the beginner stages. That's where *Intermediate Wire Weaving* comes in.

This guide offers step by step instructions that teach you more advanced weaves, including over-under, circular, and bezel wire, among others. You'll also be able to put your newfound knowledge of these weaves into practice with the projects laid out in Chapter 2. From brooch pins to ear cuffs, you'll discover a world of possibilities that will open up once you have a few weave patterns under your belt. This book will cover everything needed to successfully complete these projects, from the type of wire you need to the weaves you'll be using. If you're not familiar with what is considered to be the "beginner" weaves, I encourage you to pick up a book on beginner techniques or do some research and master the basics first. You'll understand the intermediate weaves and more difficult projects better if you have a firm grasp of the essential weaves that act as the foundation.

After you master the intermediate weaves found in this book and tackle a few projects, you'll more than likely want to take your creations to the next level by making them uniquely yours. Personalization will be discussed later on, along with common problems that you might encounter while wire weaving and how to solve them. Don't get discouraged if you find one of the projects or weaves to be more difficult than others. Mastery takes practice! There wouldn't be any fun in it if you were an expert from the get-go, would there be?

Additionally, in this book, you will learn about cold connections - how to join two pieces of metal without using heat as with soldering and welding and discover how to make your own findings.

There's a wealth of knowledge to be had in the following pages, and you'll be guided every step of the way. So roll up your sleeves, pull out your supplies, and keep reading to find out more about the art of intermediate wire weaving.

CHAPTER 1: WEAVES

Let's jump right in and talk about the weaves you'll need to progress to the intermediate projects found in this book and those that can be discovered online. Each style discussed is classic and one that is used for many creations. They will serve you well as you continue to grow your skills and learn more about wire weaving. Since you'll be practicing to start out, you can use any wire material you'd like. Copper is generally best because it's easy to handle and relatively inexpensive. You don't have to worry too much about measurements just yet, either, since we're learning how to do these weaves and not making something that requires set lengths.

Circular Weave

Also known as "coiling", this technique is particularly useful when you're working with rounded pendants and other circular items that are typically difficult to design around. While wire wrapping is generally the most popular method for forming frames around center stones, circular weaving creates intricate and visually stunning patterns that enhance the look of the entire piece.

Tools and materials needed:

- Coiling Gizmo
- 1 spool of 28 gauge round dead soft wire for base coil (you won't use the whole spool, but it's best to have more than enough when using the Coiling Gizmo)
- 24 gauge round dead soft for inner wire, cut to 30 inches
- 1 spool of 20 gauge wire (again, you won't use all of it, but it's better to have excess than to cut it too short)
- Wire cutters

Steps:

There are two ways you can do coiling, but we're going to cover the simplest method, which requires a Coiling Gizmo. These are extremely useful and relatively inexpensive. They help you create uniform coils without having to do it all by hand, which means the finished product will look more polished and professional. If you prefer to coil by hand, then that's fine, too, of course; you can skip step one and go straight to step three if you'd rather not use a gizmo.

1. Using your Coiling Gizmo, coil the 28 gauge wire until you have a piece that's about 15 inches in length. This is the main coil that you'll be weaving around a base wire.
2. If you skipped step one, your coil should already have an inner wire, and you can proceed to step three. If you used the gizmo, you'll need to thread your 24 gauge wire through the coil. You'll want this wire to be about double the length of the coiled wire, so 30 inches should be enough.
3. Pull the 24 gauge wire through until you have about 1 ½ - 2 inches sticking out from one side of the coil. Next, take your 20 gauge wire and unwind a good long piece - about 12 inches should suffice to start with. Don't cut the wire because you'll need a lot more, but you'll want to have enough to work with without it getting tangled up in excess wire.

4. Start a few inches down the 20 gauge wire so you have something to grip while you're weaving, and begin wrapping the 1 ½ - 2-inch tail from your 24 gauge wire around the 20 gauge wire. You only need to wrap a few times to secure it. Once you feel like it's secure enough, you can slide the coil up so it's flush against the 20 gauge wire.
5. Now comes the fun part. Take your 28 gauge coil and coil it around the 20 gauge wire, making sure each wrap is flush against the one before it. Keep coiling until you run out of the 28 gauge length, then take the remaining 24 gauge inner wire and wrap it around the 20 gauge a few times to secure it on that end. You can snip off the excess wire so that the lengths are equal on both ends (you should have a few inches of 20 gauge on each side). Pinch down the 24 gauge on either side so that it looks clean and polished with no wires sticking out at odd angles.

You can either stop here and use your finished coil on a project, or you can do one more coil using the 20 gauge wire and wrap it in between the 28 gauge coils so that it's sitting in the grooves. This is purely decorative and entirely optional.

Over-Over Weave

The next two weave styles are versatile in that you can use as many base wires as you want. For the over-over weave, we'll stick with three wires for the purposes of this guide, but just know that you can adjust according to your needs and project requirements.

Tools and materials needed:

- Three 20 gauge base wires (or larger if you prefer), round and dead soft
- 28 gauge weaving wire (again, can be larger or smaller based on your preference), round and dead soft
- Wire cutters

Steps:

1. Cut your three base wires as long as you wish as your only purpose is to get the hang of the weave.
2. Cut a good long length of weaving wire - between 12 and 24 inches should be enough to start with.
3. Secure your weaving wire to the bottom base wire by wrapping around once, leaving a bit of a tail to hold onto as you continue weaving.
4. With the weaving wire underneath the bottom base wire and pointing toward you, wrap it over the bottom two wires twice, making sure to slide each wrap down toward your fingers to remove any gaps.
5. Now, with the weaving wire under the middle base wire facing toward you, wrap it up over the middle and top wires twice.
6. The weaving wire will now be under all three wires facing toward you. Wrap it up over the bottom two wires again, over the top two, and continue until you're happy with the length or until you have run out of wire.

Keep in mind that you needn't only wrap the weaving wire twice; you can do it three times, five times, ten times, or as many times as you'd prefer. A simple variation such as this will give your pattern a unique look.

Over-Under Weave

Once again, you can use any number of base wires, but we'll teach you how to do this weave with six. This pattern seems complicated at first, but it's fairly straightforward and only requires that you keep track of whether you're going over or under.

Tools and materials needed:

- Six 20 gauge base wires (or larger/smaller), round and dead soft
- 28 gauge weaving wire (or larger/smaller), round and dead soft
- wire cutters

Steps:

1. Fan out your six base wires so that you have space to weave the wire in and out. There's a lot of movement to this weave, so you'll want to give yourself enough space to prevent getting tangled up.
2. Cut 12 to 24 inches of your weaving wire. Secure it by leaving a short tail for you to hold onto, and wrap it over the bottom wire.
3. Wrap your wire once around the bottom two wires going from bottom to top, ending with the wire over the top of and behind the second wire from the bottom (it might help to assign your wires numbers - bottom 1, then 2, and so on up to your top wire, 6).
4. Wrap once around base wires 2 and 3, again going from bottom to top and ending behind the third wire. Then wrap around wires 3 and 4, then 4 and 5, and finally wires 5 and 6. End with your weaving wire behind all the wires facing toward you.
5. Bring your weaving wire to the front between wires 4 and 5 and wrap once around wire 5. Then bring the weaving wire to the front between wires 3 and 4 and wrap once around wire 4. Continue following this pattern for wires 3 and 2.
6. Once you've wrapped around wire 2, bring the weaving wire down behind wire 1 and wrap up and over the bottom two wires, just like in step three.
7. Repeat step three, wrapping wires 1 and 2, 2 and 3, 3 and 4, 4 and 5, and 5 and 6.
8. Repeat step five, wrapping one wire at a time as you make your way back down.

Keep going until you're happy with the length or until you run out of wire.

Bezel Wire Weave

There are a few different weaves you can use when you're making a frame, or bezel, for a pendant necklace. Some are very basic and simple, while others are more complex and involved. The one we're going to look at is a little more intricate and on the fancier side. It forms a very sturdy frame for large stones and offers a more interesting appearance than frames created using simple wire wrapping techniques. You'll have to adjust sizing based on your specific project, but for now, we'll just go through the basic how to. In the next chapter, we'll look at some uses for these weaves and get into the nitty-gritty of tools, materials, and sizing.

Tools and materials needed:

- Three 8-inch 20 gauge base wires of round and dead soft (longer or shorter is fine; you just want enough that you can get the hang of the pattern)
- 24 inches of 28 gauge weaving wire, round and dead soft
- Wire cutters

Steps:

1. Find roughly the center of your wires, and hold onto the bunch there, fanning out the wires on the side you'll be weaving.
2. Place your weaving wire between the bottom wire and the one just above it, holding onto a small section to secure it. Wrap it once around the bottom wire going from top to bottom. Your weaving wire should now be behind the base wires facing up toward the top ones.
3. Wrap your weaving wire between the top two wires, pull it down, and then repeat (from behind, bring the weaving wire to the front between the top two wires). This creates two wraps around the bottom two wires.
4. Next, wrap the top two wires by bringing your weaving wire up and over the top, and then between the bottom two wires.
5. Wrap the top wire once by going up over the top, and then bring the weaving wire to the back by going between the top two wires.
6. Wrap around the top two wires again twice, and then wrap around the bottom two wires twice so that your weaving wire ends up in the front.
7. Make one wrap on the bottom wire as you did for the top, ending with the wire in the back and pointing down. Your pattern should look something like this so far, with the colon representing single loops:

    ||:||

    || ||: (2, 2, loop, 2, 2, loop)
8. Keep following the pattern: wrap bottom two twice, top two twice, single loop, top two twice, bottom two twice, and then loop.

There will be more steps when you're using this frame to actually make something, but for now, that's the gist of it.

Diagonal Wire Weave

When you need a simplistic but lovely design that's adaptable and can be made with as many or as few base wires as you want, a diagonal weave should be your go-to. We're going to show you how to create this pattern with two wires, but you can work up to four if you'd like.

Tools and materials needed:

- Two 8-inch 20 gauge base wires, round and dead soft or half hard
- 24 inches of 28 gauge weaving wire, round and dead soft

Steps:

1. As usual, take your two base wires and wrap your weaving wire over the bottom one to secure it. It should go front to back and end up behind the bottom wire pointing down.
2. Wrap your weaving wire over both base wires, going from the bottom to the top, then bring it between the wires and up around just the top wire.
3. Bring the weaving wire behind both wires, then pull it up and over the bottom wire, just like you did in step one. Then, wrap up and over both wires as in step two, and finish by wrapping over the top wire once.
4. Repeat the pattern: single wrap bottom, wrap both, single wrap top, and back to bottom.

This is by no means an exhaustive list of intermediate weaves. There are many techniques out there, so it would be impossible to list them all. Many of these weaves also have different names associated with them, making it even more difficult to parse them out. But you don't need to worry about any of that. Just master these weaves, and learning each one along with the beginner knowledge you already possess will be enough to help you craft incredibly detailed and stunningly simple designs. To get started using these patterns firsthand, continue on to the next (and highly anticipated) chapter - projects!

CHAPTER 2: PROJECTS

It's time to get to the good stuff. Putting your skills to good use is the most rewarding part of learning a new hobby. Wire weaving is great that way, because you get to wear or gift your finished product; Christmas and birthdays just got a whole lot easier.

All of the following projects utilize beginner weaves that you should already be familiar with as well as intermediate weaves that are covered in Chapter 1. In addition, they don't require any special tools or materials that are ridiculously expensive.

So, without further ado, let's get crafting.

Woven Bezel Pendant

Remember the bezel wire weave you just learned about in the previous chapter? Well, you already get to put it to good use.

Tools and materials needed:

- Wire cutters
- Flat or round nose pliers
- Bail making pliers
- 20 gauge copper wire, round and dead soft
- One spool 28 gauge copper weaving wire, round and dead soft
- Cabochon of the size and shape of your choosing

Steps:

1. To first figure out what length your 20 gauge base wires should be and how many you will need, take your cabochon and wrap enough wire around it so that it covers the perimeter - then triple that length. You want it to be long enough that you can use the excess length to secure the pendant and make a bail. You should also estimate how many wires you need based on the width of the sides of the cabochon. You'll generally need three or four. Once you have your measurements, cut your base wires.
2. Using the **bezel wire weave** described in Chapter 1, start in the middle of the base wires, and work your way up one side. Periodically check to make sure the frame isn't too long or larger than your stone; it needs to fit snugly or it will pop out.
3. At three points of your weave, you'll make a large loop that will be used later to secure your cabochon. These points will be at the center of the side, bottom, and the other side center of the cabochon. Once you've woven to the first point, the center of the first side, ensure you're at a point where your weaving wire is at/over the top wire. After you've woven around the top two wires and are about to make your single loop around just the top wire, use two fingers and wrap the wire around them **while** you make your single loop. All you're trying to do is leave a little slack in the wire which you'll use later.
4. Keep following the bezel weave pattern until you reach your second point at the spot where the bottom center of the stone will be. Create another loop the same way you did in the previous step. Continue

on and do the same loop on the other side center opposite the first loop. Make sure each loop is on the same base wire - (the top one).

5. Once you've woven to the correct length (the perimeter of your cabochon), set your stone down on a flat surface so that you can more easily shape your frame around it. You need to place the frame around the stone so that the loops are facing outward. Press down and pat the frame down gently so it forms around the stone. At either end of the weave where your unwoven base wires show, squeeze those wires inward so that the ends closest to the weave shape around the top of your stone. Ensure the stone can't pop through the front of the frame. We'll take care of the back soon.

6. Now it's time to close your frame. Take the front two wires on either side of the front of your frame and cross them over each other where they go into the weave. You're essentially forming an X at the very top of your frame. Bend those wires toward the back, then cross them into an X again at the back top of the frame.

7. You should still have your weaving wire coming off one side of the frame. Don't cut that off the spool yet - you're going to need it. You should also now have four base wires (two on either end of the frame) since we bent two ends out of the way. Using the same pattern we made the frame with, weave them together until you have a length that's long enough to bend around into a bail. End your weaving wire by wrapping it a few times around a single base wire, then cut it close to the base wire. Use pliers to pinch the tail down to the base wire so it's not sticking out.

8. Using bail making pliers (or your hand if you don't have any), bend the top weave over to form the standard bail shape.

9. It's now time to set the stone, so place your frame on a flat surface face down and set your cabochon in it. Take the wires you formed an X with and lay them so that they're forming an X over your stone. They don't have to be centered, but each wire should be near the loop that's on its respective side.

10. Take one of the loops that you made while weaving, flatten it out so it's no longer open, and wrap it around one of the X wires. Once you've wrapped the loop around a few times, you can cut it off and use your pliers to flatten it against the X wire. Do the same thing on the other side with the second loop. Don't cut either of the wires forming the X.

11. Cross the wires again at the bottom of the pendant and, using pliers, thread the bottom loop over and under them, wrapping the same way you did with the side wires. This will be a little more difficult since the wires are closed, but with pliers, it shouldn't be too taxing. Once you've wrapped the bottom loop around the X wires a few times, cut it and flatten it like the others. You can now cut the X wires as well. Try to loop them and tuck them in on themselves so there aren't any ends poking out.

12. Secure the wires coming from the bail by wrapping them creatively around the X wires in any way you want. You don't want to just cut them, because they're holding your bail together. At least one set should attach somewhere on the back, but the other two can be cut short and tucked under or looped over on themselves to hide the ends.

You are all finished. You now have a gorgeous pendant to show off, put on a chain, or give to someone special.

Wire Woven Brooch Pin

Brooch pins are surprisingly simple to make and can be personalized in several different ways. You can even get creative with this design and add your own embellishments.

Tools and materials needed:

- Wire cutters
- Round nose pliers
- Needle file
- 8.5 inches of 18 gauge copper round half hard wire
- 45 inches of 20 gauge copper round dead soft wire
- 12.5 feet of 26 gauge copper round dead soft wire (you may need to use more or less, depending on embellishments)
- Center stone vertically drilled, about 32mm
- Liver of sulfur and paintbrush (optional)

Steps:

1. The first thing we're going to do is make and shape the brooch pin. In this example, we'll shape it into a flower by making four petals, but you can use any shape you want. Take your 8.5-inch piece of 18 gauge wire and use your nose pliers to shape four rounded petals (or whatever design you want) on one end of the wire, leaving a nice long stem that will be the pin.
2. Take your needle file, and use it to sharpen the end of the pin. Rotate the pin as you file so the point is even. At this point, you can either add embellishments to the flower pin or move on to the bead frame.
3. For your base wires, you'll need three 12-inch pieces of 20 gauge wire. For your weaving wire, cut 45 inches of the 26 gauge wire.
4. Using either the **over-over** weave or the **diagonal** weave, start 4 inches from one end of the base wires and begin weaving. Follow your chosen pattern until you have about 4 inches of weave. If you have a center stone that's larger or smaller than the 32mm recommended, you may have to weave more or less. Once you have enough to wrap around the perimeter, shape your frame around the stone, and ensure each woven end meets at the top of the bead above the pre-drilled hole.
5. Cut 9 inches of your 20 gauge wire and use it to string the center stone, then place your stone in your frame. You'll need to thread the 20 gauge wire through the bottom of your frame so that you can secure the center stone in a later step. Leave about 1 inch of the 20 gauge wire sticking out the bottom.
6. To close the top of your frame around the bead, pinch the base wires together around the wire that's going through your stone, and use your excess wrapping wire to wrap the whole bundle. Once you're done wrapping, tuck any excess tails into the frame or wrap.
7. The next step is optional and requires a small, 5mm bead. Separate the base wires from the center wire, and use the center wire to make a few more wraps around the one you did in step 6. When you have 2 inches of wire left to wrap, string a 5mm bead so that it's facing what will be the front. Finish wrapping, then tuck in any excess wire.
8. Now we're going to use the base wires to make "wings" around the center stone. Separate them so you have three shaped into a wing on one side and three on the other. They should be spread out side to side rather than bunched up. Thread them through their respective sides of the frame, then down through the bottom of it. If you want to add beads or other embellishments to the wires sticking out

from the bottom, feel free; otherwise, you can trim them and loop them around so they wrap against the frame.

9. Now we're going to weave the wings, and, again, you have your choice of pattern. You can use any technique discussed in Chapter 1, or you can choose to go with something else you're familiar with. Start from the top and weave until you get to the back where all the frame wires meet. Trim and tuck excess wire.

10. Repeat step 9 on the other wing.

11. If you want to add any embellishments from here, go for it; otherwise, take the pin you made in the first steps and slip it through the wings behind the center stone, and you just made a brooch pin.

Braided Wire Woven Cuff Bracelet

Cuff bracelets are super easy to make, but the end result is amazing. This uses a braiding technique that's fairly beginner-level, but the use of nine base wires makes it a little more complex. Like the brooch pin, it's easily customizable; you can add beads, extra wire designs, or fancy swirls and loops - anything you want, really.

Tools and materials needed:

- 9 pieces of 10.5-inch 20 gauge round dead soft wire, either sterling silver or copper (though silver looks best with this design)
- Masking tape
- Round nose pliers
- Wire cutters

Steps:

1. Line up all nine strands of your wire and use your masking tape to hold them together on one end. Separate your wires into groups of 5 and 4 by slightly bending one group to the side and the other group to the other side.

2. Hold your wires so that the masking tape end is facing toward you and the side with five wires is on the right. Starting with the outermost wire on the right side, weave it over two wires, then under two wires to bring it over to the other side. You should now have four wires where you had five, and five wires where you had four.

3. Once again, from the left side this time, take the outermost wire and weave it over two then under two. The two wires that have been braided should now form an X towards the bottom, and you should again have five wires on the side that originally had five and four on the other.

4. Keep following this pattern of weaving over two and under two. As you progress, you'll see the bracelet starting to form a nice design of roughly diamond-shaped spaces and rounded edges. Continue weaving until you have around two inches of wire left.

5. Now it's time to finish off the ends. Don't worry if all your wire ends are different lengths. Trim the outermost wires on either side to about 1 inch, then coil them inward using your round nose pliers until they form a spiral. Curl it over the top edge of your design so that it holds the outer strands in place. Your outer wires should be coming from underneath the others, so if you curl them over they'll

secure the sides of the bracelet. Try to make both spirals level with one another.

6. Curl the rest of your wires inward using spirals to secure the ends. You don't have to do them in any particular order, as long as they all are on the same side of the bracelet.

7. Once you've finished one side, remove the masking tape from the other side and splay out your wires. If your bracelet is too short to wrap comfortably around your wrist, continue your braid on the end that had the tape. If it's long enough, cut the wires to the same lengths you had on the other side and spiral them inward just as you did in steps 5 and 6.

Now, you're done. That wasn't so hard, was it? Once you get the hang of this design, you can add beads at various intervals along the braid or even on the ends of the spirals. Get creative, and see what you can come up with.

Wire Woven Filigree Earrings

The word "filigree" might make this sound more intimidating, but it's just a fancier style that gives your earrings a delicate, almost fantasy quality. You can make the whole thing wire and not add any beads to it, but for this project, we're going to tell you how to add a small accent crystal.

Tools and materials needed:

- 4 pieces of 7-inch 20 gauge copper round dead soft wire
- 1 spool of 26 or 28 gauge copper round dead soft wire
- Round nose pliers
- 2 small crystals or beads (5mm or smaller)
- Ear wires or extra wire to make your own

Steps:

1. Start about two inches from one end of two your 20 gauge base wires. The weave we're going to use is a modified **bezel** weave. Instead of having single wraps on both the top and bottom wire, we're just going to single wrap the bottom. So, to start, wrap both wires twice, then the bottom wire **four times**. Then wrap both wires twice and the bottom wire four times. Your pattern should look something like this (dots represent single wraps):
   ||....||....||....||
2. Continue with the pattern until you have **eighteen** double wraps (||), then add **eight** single wraps to the bottom wire (........). The end weave should look like this: (||........).
3. Bend your top base wire into a tight loop so that it folds back on itself rather than forward, then realign it with the bottom base wire. The loop should be above the eight single wraps.
4. Continue on with your pattern, starting with two double wraps and four single wraps. Keep going until you have **five** double wraps, but this time don't add the four single wraps after the last double. Instead, wrap around the top wire a few times to secure your weave.
5. Using the loop you created with the base wire as your topmost point, bend the frame you've made into a U shape. Now take the side that has the most weaves (the end you started with) and, starting at the 6th double wrap, bend that end upward to form an upside down U. The 6th double wrap should be the

bottom-most point.

6. On the end you started weaving, you should have a short tail left by your weaving wire. Wrap that around a few times to secure it, and then trim it and flatten it against the base wire.

7. You should now have two base wires pointing down and two pointing up. Bend your base wires inward so that they all point toward the finished side of the frame. Trim your wires so that the innermost ones touch the inside of the frame and the outermost wires reach slightly past the frame. Curl the outermost wires so that the ends form little spirals that fit within the frame. Do the same with the innermost wires, but curl them a little tighter so that they're closer to the opposite side of the frame from the other spirals.

8. Your weaving wire should still be connected. If it isn't, you'll have to wrap a new one on. Either way, keep doing single loops (on one of the innermost wires forming a tight spiral) until you're about midway up the spiral.

9. At this point, you'll need to cut your weaving wire off the spool to make the next wrap easier. Thread the end of your weaving wire through the tight spiral so that it comes out of the back, then begin weaving around the outermost spiral that's behind the spiral you started with. Keep wrapping until your weaving wire has reached the point where the spiral touches the inner edge of the frame, then make two double wraps around both the frame and the outermost spiral to attach it. Next, return to making the single loops going around the spiral until you've reached about midway (this should only take four or five wraps). Trim and flatten/pinch down the wire.

10. To do the same on the other two spirals, cut a long length of weaving wire and follow the same wrapping pattern you did in steps 8 and 9 with one modification - when you've woven the tighter spiral to the point where it almost touches the other tight spiral, weave once around the other spiral to connect the two, then continue your single wraps.

11. Before you reach the end of the longer outermost spiral, if you want to attach a crystal, get to about midway up the outermost wire then thread your bead onto your weaving wire. Once the crystal is in between the two sets of spirals (in the middle of your earring), wrap a couple of times around the outermost spiral you already wrapped in step 9 to secure the crystal and wire in place. Then, thread it through the bead again to bring your wire back to the unfinished spiral. Keep wrapping the outermost spiral in the same way as in step 9.

12. Repeat steps 1-11 to create the second earring. Attach ear wires to both, and then you are finished.

Wire Tree Pendant

Unquestionably, one of the most iconic symbols for jewelry is the tree of life. So, it only makes sense that you should learn how to work it into your wire weaving designs.

Tools and materials needed:

- 16 gauge copper round dead soft wire (length varies based on the stone being used)
- 1 spool of 26 gauge copper round dead soft wire
- 14 pieces of 24 gauge copper round dead soft wire, with each piece double the length of your center stone
- Large center stone; 2 inches is a good size to start with

- Wire cutters
- Round nose pliers
- Bezel making pliers
- Masking tape

Steps:

1. Cut a length of 16 gauge wire that's three times the length of your center stone. Start shaping the wire around your stone by placing the bottom of your stone at the center of the wire and forming the wire around it. You should have roughly equal ends overlapping at the top of the stone, and you want the frame to be just a touch larger than your stone. Once you have the right size, bend your wires outward slightly at the top where they meet at the top of the stone. This marks your end points and where you will make the bail.

2. We're going to weave the bail first so that the frame stays in the correct shape. Make sure your base wires are separated by about a quarter of an inch or however wide you want your bail to be. Use the pattern of your choice for the bail - you can do a modified **bezel** weave, **diagonal** weave, modified **over-over**, or anything else you would like. Just as in the first project (pendant), weave until you have a long enough length that you can bend it over into a bail using your bail making pliers. Don't cut your excess wire coming from the bail just yet; you'll need them to secure the stone. Bend them into any shape that suits you, as long as it's in such a way that it will prevent the stone from popping out. You can finish off the ends into spirals if you so desire. Just make sure they're touching the frame so you can secure them to it.

3. Now, it's time for the tree. Take your 14 pieces of 24 gauge wire and hold them in a bundle so the ends are aligned. Using your round nose pliers, start twisting about a third of the way down to form the roots and bottom of the trunk. Then take smaller sections of the wire on the other side (opposite the roots) and twist them to make branches. This is where you have the opportunity to get creative, because you can make your tree look any way you want. Occasionally, you should hold your tree up to the stone to see if you like the look. Don't twist all the way to the ends of the wire as you'll need some length to secure the tree to the frame.

4. The first part you want to attach is the roots. Take a nice big piece of masking tape and lay it on the back of your frame, and then set your stone in. You should have a couple long ends of tape on either side of the frame. Use these to secure your tree down, but don't get any tape on the roots since you want to work with those.

5. Using your pliers, thread each individual root through the frame and wrap them around several times to secure them. If you made loops with the excess base wire in the back, don't forget to wrap some of the roots around those to secure them to the frame as well. When you're done, trim and tuck any root wires that are sticking out.

6. Now we're going to secure the branches. Fan them out into whatever arrangement you want, then attach the excess wire coming from the branches just as you did with the roots. Again, if your base wires are touching the frame in any place where you're securing branches, also wrap the wires around these to attach them to the frame as well. Trim and tuck the tails of any branch wires and make sure you're happy with the way the branches are arranged.

You are now done. That's all it takes to make a gorgeous and unique tree of life pendant.

Wire Woven Ring

This last project is incredibly customizable. You can use any weaving technique you want, and you will make a frame for a center stone to add on, finishing it up with some pretty spirals or really anything else.

Tools and materials needed:

- 2-3 pieces of 20 gauge copper round dead soft wire, cut to roughly 3.5 inches
- 3 feet of 28 gauge copper round dead soft wire
- Wire cutters
- Ring sizer (or just your own finger)
- Round nose pliers

Steps:

1. Starting with your 20 gauge base wires, begin wrapping the 28 gauge weaving wire in any pattern you want. The number of base wires you use depends on both the pattern you want and the width you'd like the ring to be. Feel free to exercise your creative freedom here.
2. Weave your chosen pattern until the length is long enough to wrap around into your desired ring size. You'll want to periodically check to see how you're doing, because if you weave too much, your ring will be too big. Once you've woven the proper length, finish by wrapping the weaving wire a few more times, trim it, and flatten/pinch down the tail.
3. Shape the ring around your ring shaper or another object that's the right size. Try to secure it on tightly, because you'll need something to hold the ring steady as you finish the base wire ends.
4. This is another step where you can get creative. You'll have either four or six base wire ends coming from your weave, and to close your ring, you can make loops, spirals, twisted knots, and anything else you can think of. There are so many unique ways to finish this project, so let your imagination run wild!

That's it for the projects, but hopefully, these have inspired you to start creating your own designs. Play around with different weaves and stone sizes to make entirely new creations that are 100 percent your own.

[BONUS] Donut Bail Pendant

This is very simple work and thus requires simple skill. Because of its end product, which is a whole donut bail pendant, there will be a preparative work prior to the main job. In other words, this project is a beginner one but combines simple preparatory works with the main one. The preparation is expedient because without it the foundation will not be made for the huge job. In the same vein, the main job needs a pendant so, make sure the size and type of the pendant are determined too. Make sure you follow the steps swiftly even as you read.

The following are techniques needed to finish the job:

Weaving

Downhill single Flame Stitch

Wrapping

These techniques are very basic and must have been acquired from the beginning of this book if otherwise, make sure you revise the section that deals with techniques.

Materials:

33 in. 20-gauge dead-soft copper wire

3½ ft. 24-gauge dead-soft copper wire

50mm gemstone donut

10mm large-hole copper bead

3mm bead

40 80 seed beads

Daisy spacer with a large hole

Ruler

Chain nose pliers

Round nose pliers

The following are the things to get ready before going to the main work:

Step 1

Weave a bail for a donut-shaped stone with about a large 50mm jasper donut.

Step 2

Make sure that the weave is adjustable to fit any size

Step 3

Prepare the Downhill Single Flame Stitch technique for it would be needed at the woven section.

Step 4

You will need to learn if you have not mastered how to embellish with seed beads for a dash of color and texture.

To the main project now, make sure everything needed –the techniques, materials and the pre-working stages –is ready.

Then follow the step-by-step guide below:

Step 1

Making the base wire. For the base wire, pick a 20-gauge wire and cut six pieces of it. Drop this.

Step 2

Then, pick the 24-gauge wire and cut one piece of it for the weaving wire.

Step 3

At this stage, you will need to know how much wire needed for your base stone.

Step 4

Then, Wrap a cord or string through the stone.

Step 5

Make a mark for the overlap.

Step 6

Caution needs to be taken here make sure the measurement of this length is 2½ inches.

Step 7

To complete the overlapping, add 3 in. to that measurement of the length of the base wires.

Step 8

Make a cut of six 5½ in. pieces of wire.

Step 9

Pick up the base wire #6 at the top of the Weave.

Step 10

You will need to string a 60 seed bead about 1 in. from the end of base wire 6.

Step 11

Make sure that this spacer bead makes room in the weave to add more beads later.

Step 12

Pick the weaving wire, now, place it to the right of the bead and on top of the base wire. Make sure the placement is 1 in. from the end.

Step 13

Then, at the center where both wires (base and weaving) overlapped, hold it with your left thumb and index finger.

Step 14

With everything held in the right place and proportion, wrap the weaving wire three times to the right of the bead.

Step 15

You want to prepare the base wires for weaving. Do this by doing the Downhill Wire Preparation.

Step 16

For this Downhill wire preparation, make a single Wrap.

Step 17

On base wire #1, at the bottom of the weave, string a spacer seed bead, and then complete the last wrap of the Downhill Wire Preparation.

Step 18

Remove the two spacer beads to the left and slide them back on base wires #1 and #6 to the right of the weave.

Step 19

Bring the weaving wire from behind up two base wires and go between base wires #4 and #5.

Step 20

Note that this must put you at the top of the hill as you bring the weaving wire up, over, and straight down the back, making the jump behind the weave so you can repeat the downhill pattern.

Step 21

Begin Downhill Flame Stitch Weave single wrap. At the bottom of every hill, at base wire #1, string a seed bead on base wires #1 and #6.

Step 22

You will continue with Downhill Flame Stitch Weave, stringing seed beads on base wires #1 and #6 as you go.

Step 23

Don't panic if your stitches don't want to stay in neat i.e., like in the diagonal lines because you could pinch them with chain nose pliers to make them line up.

Step 24

Now, continue the Downhill Flame Stitch Weave for the length you originally measured with the cord.

Step 25

When the weaving is completed, slide each wire out individually until the weave is centered.

Step 26

Then, wrap the weaving wire three times around base wire #6 and trim the end tightly on the back.

Step 27

You will need to push the weave into the hole of the stone and center the stone.

Step 28

With this, make a U-shaped bend to fit the stone very well. Now, remove the stone.

Step 29

You must have noticed that there are several ends that need to be finished.

Step 30

Because of this, make a 90-degree bend inward with base wires #1 and #6. They should cross each other inside the weave.

Step 31

At this stage, end base wires #2, #4, and #5 straight down on the inside of the weave, over the top of the two crossed wires. Make sure you trim all the three wires to about 3⁄8 in.

Step 32

With the round nose pliers, curl the ends of the three wires over the crossed wires to lock them in place.

Step 33

Trim the two crossed wires close, up against base wires #2 and #5.

Step 34

Repeat steps 9–11 on the other side of the weave. Put the donut back in.

Step 35

Then, with chain nose pliers, pinch the two #3 base wires that are standing straight up.

Step 36

This will bring the two sides in, right up against each other for the next step.

Step 37

Make a double wrap around one of the #3 base wires. It doesn't matter which one, as long as it is tight.

Step 38

Trim the end and pinch it down.

Step 39

On the remaining base wire, string a spacer bead, a 10mm copper bead, and a 3mm bead.

Step 40

Make a Double-Wrapped Loop at the top of these beads. If you are adding a chain as you must have planned, connect the chain to the loop before you complete the wraps.

Your work is now ready. This is a very simple way of making stunning jewelry.

Making and Installing Clasps

When ending a piece of jewelry, most notably, bracelet, necklace, etc., the clasp is what hold the two ends together. A clasp connects both ends of the piece, allowing you to open and close the piece when putting it on or taking it off while complimenting its beauty. There are quite a number of clasps designs, and this is also subject to creativity and innovation. Many types of clasps are available in the market for purchase, but you make yours. To mention but a few, we have the loop clasps, S-clasp, etc.

In this book, we will be considering how to make a few clasps and also how to install them.

1. **S-Clasp**

Materials:

Wire- two pieces of 20 gauge wire of 3cm each

Round nose pliers

Mandrel- pen (this is optional)

Steps

a. Measure and cut the stipulated amount of wire. Mark, using a marker, the 1/3 point of the wire both from ends and using a round nose plier, make a curve in the wire at each of this point to form an S shape.
b. With the tip of your round nose plier, make small loops at each ends facing outwards.
c. Now close one side tightly though cautiously. The open side serves as the clasps.

NOTE: To install this S-Clasp on a bracelet or necklace. Attach one side to one loop of the bracelet before closing it tightly. The other side will be left open, and this side gives ease of wearing.

2. The loop clasp

Materials:

Round nose plier

Wire of 5 or 6."

Steps

a. Pick the wire of 5 or 6" and use the round nose plier to bend one of the ends of the wire over to about 1.5" from the end
b. Then, make a loop by wrapping the wire ends around the pliers.
c. Then, to finish the wrapping process, hold the bottom of the pliers and complete it.
d. While making the loop, be very sure that the whole is very large to contain the hook you want to use.
e. Turn and bring the wire around and keep rolling the wire in order to make the loop center over the wire.
f. Hold the loop very well with the pliers and wrap the wire up to two to three times.
g. When the loop is fine in shape, clip close it.
h. Peradventure, the wraps are not close together and take the bent nose pliers and pinch everything up.
i. Turn the clipped end to face you, grab and hold the wire above the wrap.
j. After the grab at length, bend it towards the back
k. At this point, you will need to make the loop like the time you started. Wrap down the first wrap.
l. Now you will need to make a clip very close to the first wrap that you've bent.
m. Then, squeeze smoothly so that the ends of the clip will join together.

This is the end of your clasp. Mind you, there are many things that can be attached to this clasp. In fact, earrings can fit in very well.

CHAPTER 3: PERSONALIZING PROJECTS

The only downside to using patterns is that they're not unique or personalized if you follow them to the letter. However, as you've just seen in the projects from the previous chapter, there are endless ways you can alter a pattern or add something to it to add your own touch of creativity. Here are some ways you can personalize cookie-cutter projects without getting too complicated:

Use a Different Weave Technique

As an intermediate weaver, you now have a good number of techniques under your belt. These techniques can be modified and adapted to suit any project you're working on. Many more advanced weavers even make up their own designs as they go. Don't ever feel restricted by the weave that's suggested. If it's purely for aesthetic reasons and isn't vital to the structural integrity of the piece, change away.

Add Beads/Change the Bead Size or Style

A few of the projects in Chapter 2 either included beads or mentioned that beads could be added. You can do this with nearly any project. If the project already calls for the use of beads, you don't have to use the same size or style bead as the instructions say. Use a smaller or larger center stone, add faceted beads instead of round, and make your pieces stand out even more by including beads where the pattern does not. Just make sure you first read through the instructions thoroughly to ensure any alterations you make won't affect a later aspect of the design.

Get Creative with Your Supplies

You may not always have all the materials on hand that you need for a project. Instead of rushing out to the nearest crafting store, see if you can make do with what you have on hand. Who knows, you may end up making something you like better than you first thought you would.

Also, remember that even if a certain wire material is specified, you don't necessarily have to use that kind. If you want to use copper instead of silver or silver instead of brass (and so on and so forth), that's up to you. It is recommended that you stick with the wire hardness that the pattern suggests, though, since that will directly affect the ease with which you can weave as well as the structure of the end result.

CHAPTER 4: COMMON WIRE WEAVING PROBLEMS

No art form is without its own unique difficulties. Wire weaving, in particular, poses a few challenges for beginners and experts alike. You don't have to stress about it, though. Others have come before you and paved the way so that your own journey would be easier.

Here are five of the most common problems or questions you might encounter while wire weaving and how to solve them.

What Are Some Inexpensive but Effective Wire Choices for First Timers/Intermediate Weavers?

Perhaps the most important decision you'll make about any project is the type of wire you use. Your wire choice defines the look and ease of the project, so it's best to be informed about all your options and have a few tried and tested options that you regularly turn to.

A surprising discovery made by many people just getting into wire weaving is that there are more wire options than expected. Some of the most common metals used in jewelry making are copper, aluminum, nickel, brass, sterling silver, and iron. Many metals can be made in different colors like the traditional gold and silver using filling and plating processes.

For beginner and intermediate weavers alike, copper is often the ideal choice. It's inexpensive and easy to work with, plus it makes beautiful designs and is readily available in a wide range of gauges.

Another option is pure or fine silver wire. It's less prone to breaking than sterling silver and thus is much easier (and less frustrating) to work with.

How Do I Stop Overworking and Mangling My Base Wires?

Your base wires are the framework of your weaving project and will either make your life easier or cause you endless headaches. Handling them takes practice, but there are a few things you can do to speed up the learning process.

1. Be sure you cut the right length for your project. Too short, and you'll be struggling to weave too much wire on limited space; too long, and you'll have extra wire tripping you up and making you fumble around. Both scenarios lead to mangled base wires as you try to work around the lack or excess.
2. Relax your grip. When we're working with small tools and tiny wires, we have a tendency to tense up and hold our base wires like they're slippery eels. Switch to a firm but gentle grip that won't leave your hand tired and your wires bent out of shape.
3. Use the right gauge base wires. Most projects will call for 18 gauge, because this is an easy size to work with, and you can create many different weave patterns using it. If your base wires feel flimsy or soft, double check the gauge. Your problem could be as simple as mislabeled packaging or an unintentional switch.

How Can I Make Wire Weaving Easier on My Hands?

Jewelry making is a hands-on business. Your poor palms and chapped fingers will be begging for a break before too long if they haven't already; however, your solution doesn't have to be to stop and step away from the crafting table for a few days. On the contrary, if you stop working with your projects for too long, not only will you lose motivation, but you'll also find that it hurts more when you come back to it. Just as guitar players develop calluses from their guitar strings, you will develop jewelry maker calluses; wear them proudly.

Of course, you don't have to accept the pain. One option you can use if you want to avoid calluses or have painful ones already is to wrap your fingers in medical tape or bandages to prevent the wire from rubbing against your skin. You can also use lotion to soothe and soften your hands.

Aside from calluses, cramping and carpal tunnel are also problems that could develop when you work with thin wires and perform repetitive motions. One way to counter this is to take frequent breaks while you're working on a project to let your hands rest and try not to hold the wires in a vice grip. You can also perform hand and finger strengthening exercises - the rest of your body gets stronger when you work out, so why shouldn't your extremities?

Is There a Way to Oxidize Metal Without Liver of Sulfur?

If you don't already know, liver of sulfur is used to give an antique look to jewelry by oxidizing it, which means the metal is chemically combined with oxygen. It reacts with the metal in a way that causes it to take on a darkened appearance. What if you don't want to use chemicals, though? What if the smell of liver of sulfur makes you sick? It's not the most pleasant smell, after all.

There are other ways to oxidize metals. Here are a few:

1. You can use boiled eggs, surprisingly enough. Yes, it does sound disgusting, and no, this probably wouldn't be your first choice, but if you're ever in a pinch or want a cheaper way to add patina, boil a couple of eggs, crush them up in a bag with the shells, and let the metals you want oxidized sit in the bag with the mixture for as long as it takes to darken them to the stage you want.
2. You can also soak the metal in white vinegar along with hydrogen peroxide and salt, though in some cases hydrogen peroxide alone might be enough.

How and Where Can I Substitute Silver Wire with Copper Wire?

When you're learning a new weave or trying a new design for the first time, you'll more than likely choose copper as your material. However, when you're looking to gift your creations or even sell them, when is copper okay and when should silver be your first choice?

One big issue with copper is that if it oxidizes or you do it yourself to create an antique look, the patina or tarnish can rub off onto the skin of the wearer. This gives skin a green tinge, which can be disconcerting.

If you want to use copper wire in place of silver, keep in mind who will be wearing it, what part of the body the piece will be on, and if the majority of the piece is made from copper or just some of it. If you're making wire woven earrings, for example, the only part you need to worry about coming into contact with the skin is the ear wire. If the earring is copper but the wire is something like stainless steel, you should have no problem.

CHAPTER 5: HOW TO MAKE YOUR OWN FINDINGS

Wire is good for more than just weaving! You can also use it to make your own findings. This not only saves money, but it allows you to make your designs even more unique. Wouldn't you like to be able to say your piece is 100 percent handmade, findings and all? While there are some findings you will want to buy just because they're intricate or difficult to make, there's no reason you can't start making the following right away.

Jump Rings

Jump rings are essential in various designs. While you can buy them from any craft store, why bother if you already have oodles of wire around?

The size of your jump rings and the gauge of wire you use will vary depending on the project, but to try your hand at it to see if you prefer making your own, follow these steps:

1. Using 18 gauge round copper wire, make coils with either a Coiling Gizmo (using a thicker rod) or by wrapping the wire around something round that's the correct thickness for the rings you're making.
2. Using wire cutters, trim the ends of your coil so that they're even with the rest of the coil and aren't sticking out at odd angles. You want the cuts to be smooth, because if you look at most jump rings, the open ends are both flat so they can fit together easily.
3. Loosen the whole coil, then take your wire cutters and cut your first ring at the second coil in the spot where the end of the first coil is. This makes more sense once you have the coil in front of you. It's fairly simple to know where to cut to make the proper jump ring shape.
4. Cut all the coils in the same manner, and there you have it. You've made your own jump rings and can now experiment with different gauges and sizes.

Hook Clasps

Many handmade bracelets close with a hook clasp. Oftentimes, though, you can only get these in sets of two or three, and they're way more expensive than they should be. Both of those problems go away if you make your own.

1. Using 16 gauge round dead soft wire, cut about 2.75 inches off and use a jewelry file to smooth down both ends nicely.
2. Make a loop on one end of the wire using round nose pliers. Try to make the loop as wide as the widest part of your pliers.
3. At the other end of the wire, take about a quarter of an inch of the wire and bend it up at a 90-degree angle in the opposite direction of your curled loop.
4. Find the center of the wire between the loop and the 90-degree angle. Using your pliers, bend that same direction you bent the angle to form a rectangle that has about a quarter-inch opening between the bent angle and the straight part of the wire. The rectangle and the loop should be on the opposite side.

This is a fairly simple hook clasp. Feel free to play around with it to come up with different methods and designs.

Ear Wires

There are so many different types of ear wires, but a few of the most popular are lever backs, french hooks, and kidney wires. All you need to make your own are pliers and a few inches of 20 gauge wire in the metal you like best. Keep in mind that copper can cause discoloration, so you may want to stick with sterling silver.

All you really need to do is bend the wire into the proper shape, which you can do by looking online to find a shape you like; you can also use a pair of your own earrings as a reference.

Which Pieces You Should Still Buy

As mentioned previously, there are some findings that take more work than they're worth, including the following:

- Crimps
- Pin backs
- Bead tips
- Crimp covers
- Bead caps

Thankfully, all of these supplies are relatively cheap and easy to find.

CHAPTER 6: COLD CONNECTIONS

You know the image of the burly blacksmith hammering away at metals heated to astonishing temperatures and forging massive swords fit for warriors? It turns out that that's not the only way to connect two or more pieces of metal. While metalsmithing and forging are exciting hobbies, they're a little too much work for someone who's just getting into the art of jewelry making. If you're new to working with metals or don't have a lot of experience crafting, take your time to learn the processes that come before the more labor-intensive techniques.

To join pieces of metal, you can either use warm connections, such as soldering and welding, or you can use cold connections. We're going to focus on cold connections, but don't let the name fool you. Just because these methods don't involve heat doesn't mean that they aren't effective and durable.

There are two different types of cold connections: pierced and adhered. Both types incorporate a few different techniques which are explained in more detail below. One isn't necessarily better than the other. It all depends on the project you're working on, the tools available to you, and the look you want the finished product to have. Before you can decide, however, you need to know what each entails.

Pierced Cold Connections

Despite the name, pierced cold connections do not necessarily have to be pierced. There are two main techniques: riveting and wireworking. You should be very familiar with wireworking by now, because wire weaving is a type of wireworking. There are a few others that are discussed below, but first, we'll look at the different rivets and how to use them.

Riveting

Riveting may sound like a complicated process, but it's actually straightforward. If the piece you're working with already has holes or you plan to add holes, rivets are probably going to be your best bet. There are many different types of rivets including eyelets, semi-tubular, and nail-head, and they're separated into two categories: open rivets and solid rivets. The rivet you choose will depend on your project and personal preference. Open rivets typically feature a tube that allows for the use of jump rings and other connectors or wire, while solid rivets don't.

The tools you need may vary depending on the type of rivet you use, but in general, you will need the following:

- Riveting hammer
- File and/or wire cutters
- Bench block
- Drill set

If you don't want to purchase and try out a bunch of different rivets to decide which you like best, you can always go old school and use wire to make wire rivets. Since you're already learning wire weaving and are familiar with the various gauges and metals, this might be the best option to start out with, although it's a bit more labor-intensive. For this method, you'll need the tools listed above, plus the metals you want to join, along with wire that fits into the holes you already have drilled or intend to drill. The wire should fit snugly; this will be a solid rivet. Detailed instructions on how to make wire rivets can be found online, but here's a quick run-through:

1. Cut enough wire so that 0.5 to 1mm will be left on either side of the joined metal.
2. Make sure that your wire fits the holes that you have drilled in your metal pieces and that the ends of the wire are flat and smoothed out. If they're uneven, your rivet will be messy and could have sharp edges.
3. Set the metal with the inserted wire on your bench block (steel is best). Using your riveting hammer, tap on the top of the wire on one side, then flip the piece over and do the same on the other side. You're trying to sandwich the metal between the flattened tops of the wire, so you'll probably have to repeat this process a few times to ensure the metals are tight together and that the wire is smooth and domed on either side.

It's as easy as that. Of course, the first few times you try this, it won't be so simple. Start out with cheap materials that you can practice with until you get your technique down. Alternatively, you can use nail-head rivets, which come with one side pre-hammered so that all you have to do is tap down the other side instead of both sides - but where's the fun in that?

Wireworking

As already mentioned, wire weaving is a type of wireworking because it involves the use of wire to create a solid item. Other methods of wireworking include wire wrapping and wire stitching. Since you're already familiar with wire weaving, we're going to take a closer look at the other two.

Wire wrapping is a very popular technique that is often used with stones to make beautiful and unique necklaces and earrings. It's similar to wire weaving, except it doesn't make use of base wires and typically involves a focal piece such as a gemstone or pendant. Basic wire wrapping starts with a frame that goes around the edges of the center stone being wrapped. To make the frame, you'll usually need the following items:

- 20 gauge square soft wire
- 22 gauge half-round hard wire
- Wire cutters
- Flat nose pliers
- Tape
- Felt tip pen
- Ruler

While some steps may vary from project to project, here is how a basic frame is made:

1. Cut six pieces of the 20 gauge wire measuring about 8 inches (though the length may vary depending on the center stone size). These are your main frame wires that will go around the perimeter of the

stone.

2. Line up the six pieces side by side and tape them together at the ends. You want them all to be as even as possible, since in the next step you'll be binding them to create a solid frame.
3. Use your felt tip pen to draw a line through the center of the frame (this will be at about 4 inches). The line represents your first binding site.
4. Cut a 5-inch piece of the 22 gauge wire. This is your binding wire.
5. Wrap the binding wire around the center mark you made on the frame using your flat nose pliers. There should be equal lengths of binding on either side of the mark, and the wraps should be snug up against one another so no gaps show.
6. Measure out a quarter-inch from the edge of the binding on either side and then another quarter-inch from each of those lines. In between the two lines you just drew on either side of the middle binding, you're going to repeat step 5. You should have a total of three bindings wrapped around the frame.

The steps can vary greatly from this point, but this should provide you with a place to start. From here, you can add your stone and let your imagination run wild as you design intricate loops and curls around the centerpiece and along the frame. There are endless ways to go from here, so play around with it and see what you can create.

Wire stitching is a lot more complex and is beyond the scope of this book, but there are many resources out there if you want to give it a try. It essentially involves joining rows of beads using stitch-like patterns, but with wire instead of thread.

Adhered Cold Connections

The name alone is fairly self-explanatory. Adhered cold connections make use of bonding materials to hold pieces of metal together. Don't underestimate the power of adhesion; jewelry-grade materials are made to be durable and stick to smaller surface areas. It's like soldering, only without heat. The two most common bonding materials used by jewelers are glue and clay.

Glue

This isn't your typical Elmer's glue that kids use to make macaroni art. Jewelry glue is tough, but it also allows you to create professional quality pieces because it's designed not to look tacky. With the right application techniques, no one will even be able to tell it's there.

Some tips for applying jeweler's glue include the following:

- Prepare your metal surfaces by sanding them so the glue has something to hold onto.
- A little goes a long way. Start off with less than you think you'll need and add more from there.
- Most glues need time to set, so ensure you have some sort of clamping mechanism to avoid having to manually hold the pieces together until you're sure they've adhered.

The three most popular (and effective) jewelry glue includes E-6000, Gorilla Glue, and Devcon Epoxy. E-6000 is thick and flexible, and it's useful in that it doesn't dry immediately, meaning you can make adjustments after applying it so that it sets in just the way you want it to. Gorilla Glue takes several hours to dry and should only be used when you need an extra strong connection. Devcon Epoxy can be found in both 2 -minute and 30-minute set time formulas, but be careful with either one, because the materials will generally bind right away and will be more difficult to adjust than those with E-6000.

Clay

While there's no decorative element provided by glue, clay, on the other hand, can be used to not only create a cold connection, but also enhance the visual appeal of a piece. It can be especially effective if you're working with delicate metals with a very small surface area that is too difficult to glue. Kato Polyclay and Vitrium Clay are the standard choices, and both offer color options that expand the possibilities depending on how unique your pieces are. Vitrium Clay is also available translucent if you want to keep things simple.

One thing to keep in mind is that while Vitrium will air dry, Kato Polyclay needs to be baked in order to cure, so it's not a purely cold method of connection. On the plus side, you can use it for more than just adhering metals. There's a big market for handcrafted beads, and with polyclays, you can come up with your own designs.

CHAPTER 7: SUPPLIERS AND RESOURCES

Nothing in this book would be possible without the right supplies and resources. If you're at an intermediate stage, you probably already have a cache of supplies, but it doesn't hurt to know where to shop in the future. It's an unfortunate truth that many local craft stores are far too expensive to sustain a hobby, and that's where online retailers come in. A few standout options have made a name for themselves in the jewelry-making world. If you don't already know about them, below we have detailed some places you should look into.

Rio Grande

If you talk to any wire weaver about where they get their supplies, they'll more than likely start waxing poetic about Rio Grande. Based out of New Mexico, Rio Grande offers chains, findings, packaging, organizers, tools, metals, and practically anything else you could possibly need to start any craft you wish. They've become dependable for their excellent prices and quality supplies.

MonsterSlayer

Also based out of New Mexico, MonsterSlayer has an incredibly vast inventory of not just wire, but every kind of jewelry supply need out there. Their website isn't the most user-friendly, but if you need an obscure metal or are looking for some really unique items, you should definitely take a look on MonsterSlayer's site.

Alibaba

You can't be in the jewelry world and not know about Alibaba. They offer bulk goods in every category, including jewelry supplies. The shipping times are a bit long (sometimes over a month), but the quality is surprisingly good and the prices are phenomenal. If you want a lot of supplies for the price of a few, Alibaba is your best bet.

Etsy

While Etsy is marketed as the place to find handmade goods, it also has excellent supply stores. Sure, the prices aren't the lowest, but if you need something fast or are looking for supplies that might not be sold elsewhere, it's worth looking on Etsy. Besides, if you one day decide you want to sell your wire woven creations, it helps to know the system and establish a relationship with a trusted supplier.

CONCLUSION

Congratulations on getting to the end of *Intermediate Wire Weaving*! By now, you've learned a few new weaves, put those weaves to the test with some fun projects, discovered how to personalize future projects, and gained some knowledge about other jewelry making techniques that will help you make even more amazing creations in the future.

Don't worry if it didn't all make sense on the first go. Even though you're past the beginner stages, there's still a lot to learn, and it does get more difficult from here. Never give up, though. Above all else, wire weaving is supposed to be fun. If you're pressuring yourself to make perfect designs the first time, learn a new weave as fast as possible, or if you are generally turning the process into a chore, you'll lose interest before long. The best way to avoid this is to leave perfection out of the equation. Mistakes often lead to innovation, so don't be afraid to make a few; they might just turn into your best pieces.

From here, keep practicing the weaves from Chapter 1, and add some personalized touches to the projects in Chapter 2. There's a world of possibilities open to you now, so set out those wires, get some stones ready, roll up your sleeves, and just weave!

METRIC CONVERSION CHART

Length Conversion Table of Common Length Units

	Millimeter (mm)	Centimeter (cm)	Meter (m)	Kilometer (km)	Inch (in)	Foot/ feet (ft)	Yard (yd)
1 millimeter (mm)	1	0.1	0.001	0.000001	0.39370078740157	0.0032808398950131	0.00109361329833377
1 centimeter (cm)	10	1	0.01	0.00001	0.39370078740157	0.032808398950131	0.0109361329833377
1 meter (m)	1000	100	1	0.001	39.370078740157	3.2808398950131	1.0936132983377
1 kilometer (km)	1000000	100000	1000	1	39370.078740157	3280.8398950131	1093.6132983377
1 inch (in)	25.4	2.54	0.0254	0.0000254	1	0.083333333333333	0.0277777777777778
1 foot / feet (ft)	304.8	30.48	0.3048	0.0003048	12	1	0.33333333333333
1 yard (yd)	914.4	91.44	0.9144	0.0009144	36	3	1

Wire conversion Chart

Gauge	Inches	Millimeters
10	0.102	2.59
11	0.091	2.31
12	0.081	2.06
13	0.072	1.83
14	0.064	1.63

15	0.057	1.45
16	0.052	1.29
17	0.0045	1.14
18	0.04	1.02
19	0.0036	0.91
20	0.032	0.81
21	0.028	0.71
22	0.025	0.64
23	0.023	0.58
24	0.02	0.51
25	0.0179	0.455
26	0.0159	0.404
27	0.0142	0.361
28	0.0126	0.32
29	0.0113	0.287
30	0.01	0.25
31	0.0089	0.226
32	0.008	0.2
33	0.0071	0.18
34	0.0063	0.16
35	0.0056	0.142
36	0.005	0.13
37	0.0045	0.114
38	0.004	0.1

The conversation given here is strictly on the measurement used throughout the book. Apply your calculation using a calculator where necessary. Note that while measuring the wires, the centimeter and millimeter gauge of the wire could be used too with a ruler.

RESOURCES

Anderson, J. (2010, June 08). Woven Wire Ring Tutorial. Retrieved from https://www.youtube.com/watch?v=iQ-Az7jIeFA

Klingenberg, R. (n.d.). Easy Wire Hook Clasp (Tutorial). Retrieved from https://jewelrymakingjournal.com/easy-wire-hook-clasp-tutorial/

Knaus, T. (n.d.). Wire-woven brooch. Retrieved from http://www.facetjewelry.com/metal-wire/projects/2016/05/wire-woven-brooch

Making an Ear Wire. (n.d.). Retrieved from https://www.fusionbeads.com/making-an-ear-wire

OxanaCrafts. (2016, July 02). Framed Tree Of Life Cabochon Pendant Wire Wrap Tutorial. Retrieved from https://www.youtube.com/watch?v=gfJPosJWikw

OxanaCrafts. (2016, May 20). Wire Wrap Tutorial Filigree Crystal Earrings. Retrieved from https://www.youtube.com/watch?v=hindW3ISnfU

OxanaCrafts. (2016, July 01). Wire Wrapped Coiled Pendant Tutorial (Cabochon). Retrieved from https://www.youtube.com/watch?v=APb48z6c9d0

Van Look, B. (n.d.). Jewelry-Making Articles. Retrieved from https://www.firemountaingems.com/resources/jewelry-making-articles/c12a

CHAIN MAILLE WIRE WEAVING

How to Make Chainmaille with Affordable Metals and Minimal Tools

INTRODUCTION

Chain maille is also called maille or chain mail. It refers to the jewelry or armor made by joining jump rings to each other.

Maille is a French word that means 'mesh.' To make something using chain maille you will follow steps such as:

- Wrapping a metallic wire around one mandrel and making a coil
- Cutting the coil to make jump rings
- Then linking the rings to one another in a particular pattern using pliers to open and close them

History

Chain maille is amongst the earliest types of metallic armor. It is estimated that the oldest surviving maille armor was made 2700 years ago. It was found in the Celtic warriors' graves. Similar armors were also found in Scythia, which can be dated back to the fifth century B.C.

The armor was lightweight and could resist slashing and piercing. It was commonly used by the Romans, Celts, Persians, Japanese, and the Europeans.

Most of the historical pieces of chain maille are armors. But the ancient Egyptians and Vikings also made chain maille jewelry.

Popularity

In recent years, chain maille has become very popular. Besides using it for armor, artists have started giving it preference when making chain maille jewelry, some of them even make sculptures with it. Chain maille's versatility is remarkable; artists have made chess boards, baskets, sunglass lenses, belts, and dresses out of this superb medium. Chain maille artwork includes ornaments, macramé, wall hangings, and headdresses.

The patterns formed by linking rings are known as weaves. Stability is very crucial for things like shark suits where the metal rings are riveted closed or soldered so that the rings do not open on the application of force.

However, it is different in the case of jewelry where the rings are just twisted and closed. So the jewelry can be created more quickly and can also be modified in the future.

It is possible to make maille from almost any material, which can be shaped into a ring or circle. That means most of the metals, and even rubber, which is not traditionally used for jewelry, can be used for it.

There are more than a thousand chain maille patterns that are known. This is very impressive. Weavers can even create their own designs. People make simple maille chains to complex maille sheets.

If you are interested in making chain maille jewelry but do not want to spend too much on your hobby, this book will show you how to make chain maille without splurging on gold or silver.

And with that, happy chain mailling!

CHAPTER 1: UNDERSTANDING THE BASICS OF CHAIN MAILLE

Jump Rings

Jump rings are the basic things that are required to create chain maille. There are a wide variety of rings made from different metals that can be used for chain maille. You can choose whatever suits your budget and tastes.

The metals that are usually used are copper, aluminum, sterling silver, titanium, niobium, and stainless steel. Besides this, some people also use brass, bronze, and gold-fill. Nowadays, anodized and dyed metals are also very popular.

The jump rings are slightly open at the ends. You should look at those ends and see how flush they are.

There are two types of jump rings. One is called 'saw-cut' and the other is called 'machine cut.' When you are making chain maille jewelry you must always use saw cut jump rings. The machine cut rings have angles on them and they are not flush cut.

Understanding the ring names

The jump rings sold by some suppliers are named with a series of letters followed by numbers. The letter indicates the ring's ID, or inner diameter, and the number tells the gauge of the wire.

The letters are arranged in alphabetical order. So size B is significantly smaller compared to size X. The letters indicate the mandrel size that was used to make the rings by wrapping the wire around it.

The thickness of the wire or the wire gauge may be a bit difficult to understand at first because the larger numbers indicate that the wire is thin while the smaller numbers stand for thicker wires. For example, a 20 gauge wire is thinner than a 14 gauge wire.

Different systems of numbering are used according to the kind of metal. To make it every more complicated, many chain maillers feel that it is better to use the measurements of just the wire instead of using gauges. They do so with the thought that customers will prefer to know the exact size of the wire.

So when you buy jump rings make sure you know how the particular supplier measures the rings. Find out if they measure it in terms of inner diameter (ID), or outer diameter (OD). Some of them may measure it in inches or millimeters. Moreover, some suppliers may use AWG, SWG, or possibly both. Therefore, you should ask the supplier for the correct measurements of the rings, taking into consideration the springback, which we will discuss in the following section.

Springback

When you wrap a wire around the mandrel to make jump rings, the wire relaxes a little after it is coiled, this occurrence is called springback.

The springback is different for each metal. For instance, if a ring is formed by wrapping one stainless steel wire around one 5/16" mandrel, it will be comparatively much bigger than a ring formed by wrapping sterling wire around the same mandrel. The reason for this is that steel is tougher, so it goes back more to its original position; that is, it remains straighter.

Another thing to keep in mind is that even if you use the same material, with different gauges, when you wrap them around an identical mandrel their IDs will be different as springback depends on their gauge.

Besides this, various suppliers use different methods to wrap the wire around the mandrel. So even if the metal and the wire gauge are the same, the springback may be different.

Moreover, if the temper of the wires is different (even if they are the same material and the same mandrel are used) the springback may also be different

Springback has an influence on the aspect ratio. Therefore, it must be taken into consideration while buying rings.

Temper

Temper refers to the softness or hardness of the wire. If the wire is soft it will be more malleable. If it is hard, it will be more stiff and durable. Some examples of temper are Full Hard, Half Hard, and Dead Soft.

Ring size

When you buy jump rings you should ask the supplier if they are referring to the inner diameter or the outer diameter, because it makes a big difference!

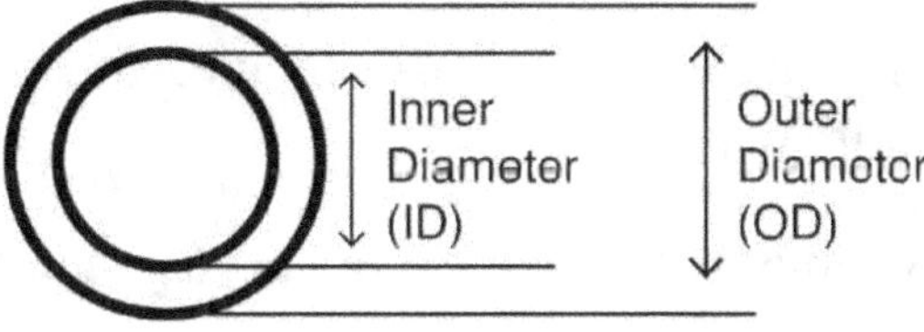

[1]

Inner diameter

The size of a ring is actually the inside diameter of a ring. It is measured mostly in fractions such as 3/8 inch, 1/2 inch, and 7/16 inch. The actual measurements may vary, for example, 1/2 inch sized ring could be 0.483 inches or 0.561.

---

[1] Beaded Jewelry Diva. (2015, August 24). Chain Maille 101 - Intro to chain mail jewelry, part 1. Retrieved from

https://www.youtube.com/watch?v=_thIHKyOEGs&list=PLlrjOezwxajahk4CyWK_ytjjN2HKbIteS&index=4&t=0s

The inner diameter refers to the distance between the two ends of the inside part of the ring. It is the space inside the ring. For example, if someone says that the ID is 5 mm it means that the inner space is 5 mm.

Outer diameter

The OD is measured from one outer end of the ring to the other outer end. It can be measured correctly with the help of calipers when the rings are closed. Usually, maille purists do not give the size of a ring in OD. For example, if someone says the OD is 5 mm it means the total size of the ring is 5 mm. Companies that supply beads, however, tend to measure them in OD because they are accustomed to that method when working with beads.

In-between the inner and outer diameters, there is a wire. It is important to know the diameters because the relationship between the wire thickness and the inner diameter determine the aspect ratio.

Aspect ratio is equal to the inner diameter divided by the thickness of the wire. For example, for an 18 gauge ring with a 4mm ID and a 1mm wire thickness, the aspect ratio or AR is equal to four. Here is another example to be sure you follow, for a 16 gauge ring with a 4mm ID and a wire thickness of 1.26, the aspect ratio is equal to 3.1.

Even two rings of the same gauge can have different aspect ratios. For example, if there are two 18 gauge rings, a smaller ring may have an AR of 3.4 and a larger one may have an AR of 5.9. When you put other rings through these two rings you can see that it is possible to put more rings through the ring that has an AR of 5.9 than the ring that has an AR of 3.4.

Wire Gauge

Just like an electrical wire, the gauge of the metallic wire used for making rings refers to the wire's thickness. The wire with a higher gauge is thinner than the wire that has a lower gauge. The typical gauges of wire that are used for chain maille are 14 gauge, 16 gauge, 18 gauge, and 20-gauge.

Wire diameter or WD refers to the wire's thickness. It is usually measured in gauges. However, some maillers mention it in decimals of inches or millimeters.

Gauge measurement is different for various metals. For example, 16 gauge sterling is not the same as 16 gauge steel.

12-gauge to 16 gauge is mainly used for armor chain maille, 16 gauge to 22-gauge is used for jewelry, and 22-gauge to 24-gauge is used for micro maille.

American wire gauge

There are different ways of measuring wire gauge. The American Wire Gauge is mostly used for jewelry in the United States. According to this 18 gauge is roughly 1.02 mm in diameter.

This numbering system is used for metals that do not contain iron known as non-ferrous metals. Traditionally, it has been used for copper and sterling silver.

Standard wire gauge

There is another system called the Standard Wire Gauge, which is used extensively outside the U.S. This system is generally used for measuring jump rings used for chain maille and armor.

This numbering system is also referred to as the Imperial Wire Gauge. It is used for metals that contain iron, known as ferrous metals. Usually stainless steel is measured using this number system. However, it is better to ask the supplier about the exact size of the rings.

Difference between the two systems

Any ring measuring within 20-gauge in the American system will be one size bigger than that measured in the Standard system.

Another difference between the American and Standard systems of measurement is that the former measures in millimeters and the latter measures in inches.

So when you buy the rings you must keep these points in mind. Your gauges will have a huge influence on the item you are making.

Aspect Ratio

Aspect ratio refers to a value that compares the inner diameter of a ring with a wire's (of which it has been made) diameter.

In other words, aspect ratio is the relationship between the thickness of the wire and the space inside the ring.

For example, if a piece of 4-in-1 weave is made using 22-gauge 4mm rings and has an aspect ratio of 4.3, and another piece is made of 14 gauge 10mm rings and has an aspect ratio of 4.1, even though there is not much difference between their aspect ratios you can see that the ring size, wire thickness, and the end result are significantly different. The thing that remains the same, however, is the relationship between the thickness of the wire and the space within the ring.

This shows how valuable aspect ratio is for chain maille weaving.

You should remember this rule: The higher the aspect ratio number is, the more space exists inside the ring.

In other words, if the aspect ratio of a ring is high you can fit more rings into it. If the aspect ratio of a ring is less not many rings can fit into it. The number of rings you can fit into another ring is important in that if the aspect ratio is high the chain maille weave is loose; if the AR is lower the weave is tight.

The formula for calculating aspect ratio is:

$$AR = ID / WD$$

Where Aspect Ratio = Inner Diameter of the ring divided by the Wire Diameter

Importance of aspect ratio

Finding the AR of the jump ring is crucial because some designs might look better or worse depending on the AR. Moreover, it is helpful to know the AR because it forms the basis of knowing which weaves can be made with a particular ring.

For example, if you are familiar with the AR for one ring, which you have already used for making a design and now you want to make a similar bigger or smaller design, you can simply use a smaller or larger diameter of gauge rings that have a similar AR of your previous project.

Examples of a few aspect ratios

Here are some examples of aspect ratios that are suitable for particular weaves.

AR Chart for Different Weaves of Chain Maille [2]

Weave	Typical Aspect Ratio
European 4-1	4.0 - 6.0
European 6-1	4.5 - 6.5
Full Persian	5.5 - 6.5
Half Persian 3-1	4.0 - 5.5
Half Persian 4-1	5.0 - 6.5
Jens Pind Linkage (JPL)	3.0
Byzantine	3.5 - 4.5

There is one theoretical minimum AR below which a weave does not work. You can make most of the weaves with larger aspect ratios (although some of them like JPL, may become unstable). However, after a certain

---

[2] Aspect ratio and ring sizing. Retrieved from

http://www.chainmaildude.com/store/index.php?route=information/information&information_id=10

point, they tend to be less aesthetically appealing.

The Best Metal to Use

Aluminum, bronze, copper, stainless steel, brass, sterling silver, titanium, niobium, and yellow gold (10k solid) can be used for making chain maille jewelry. But anodized aluminum jump ring specs are ideal for it.

Certain metals like titanium and niobium are dipped in solutions that are electrically charged and the voltage is modified to create dazzling colors. This process is referred to as anodizing.

Benefits of anodized aluminum

It is easy to clean and maintain jewelry made out of anodized aluminum. You can simply put the item in soapy, warm water for some minutes. You should not use any harsh detergents for cleaning it. Use some mild soap to remove the oil and dirt that may have accumulated on it. After that, rinse it properly and allow it to air dry. When it is completely dry, you can put it in a plastic bag and store it, so that it is not exposed to the various elements.

That said, if you gently wipe the piece with a soft cloth when you are done wearing it, you might only have to clean the piece thoroughly twice a year.

You should not use any abrasive materials to clean your piece because these materials can damage the colorful oxide layer. Avoid using Brasso or silver polishes. Do not rub it against any hard surfaces while cleaning or put it through any ultrasonic cleaner.

Jewelry made with anodized aluminum is light as well as durable.

You can add color to the chain maille projects in the most inexpensive way by using anodized aluminum rings.

Difference between anodized and bright aluminum

Aluminum is a very common element. The rings that are used for making jewelry are made from an alloy that is made up of 92.9% aluminum mixed with manganese, and a bit of chromium, iron, copper, silicon, titanium, and zinc manganese.

Aluminum that is not dyed and is silvery in color is referred to as bright aluminum. Generally aluminum is not very bright but the aluminum rings become highly polished and bright after a process called tumbling.

Anodized aluminum jump rings are formed by enduring an electrolytic bath with dyes and then a specific amount of electrical current is applied to them. After anodizing, the dye binds chemically with the aluminum. Moreover, anodizing makes the metal harder.

Difference between anodizing, plating, and enameling

Anodizing is different from plating and enameling. Plating refers to a thin metallic coating on another substance made of metal. For example, copper is plated with silver. Enameling refers to the non-metallic coating on a metal. For example, enameled copper is coated with plastic.

Anodizing refers to the method of changing the metal's surface using one electrochemical process. In this procedure the metal's composition does not change. An electric current is passed through a metal, such as titanium and niobium, to anodize it. The current creates a layer of oxide on the metal's surface. The voltage that is applied determines how thick the layer of oxide will be and its color.

The process for anodizing aluminum is a bit different than others. When the electric current is passed through aluminum, instead of forming one oxide layer it makes tiny holes on its surface. The hole size depends on how much voltage is applied. In turn, the hole size determines which color pigment can fit into the holes. Different sizes of small blobs make up each color. One protective coating has to be applied after applying the pigment to lock it in and protect from the various elements.

How to Open and Close Jump Rings

In order to make your jewelry in a professional manner it is essential to know how to close jump rings perfectly.

When you want to open a jump ring do not pull it to the opposite sides. You should twist it and open it. When you want to close the ring, twist and push the sides towards the other end so that they are joined properly.

Step 1

Hold one jump ring using two pliers. You can use chain nose, bent nose, or flat nose pliers for this purpose. One plier should on the left and the other should be on the right of the opening or cut on the ring.

Step 2

To open a jump ring you should bring the tip of one of the pliers towards yourself. Push the tip of the second plier to the other side, away from yourself.

Step 3

When you want to close a jump ring you should reverse this process. You should bring the two end parts of the open jump rings inwards and take them past one another. Then push them back and make them sit perfectly against each other. This way the joint will look neater.

CHAPTER 2: GETTING STARTED

Now that you are familiar with all the terms related to chain maille, it is time to go shopping. We will you to make the right choices in your purchasing.

Anodized Aluminum Jump Ring Specs

You can directly buy anodized aluminum jump ring specs instead of wasting your money on buying a whole bunch of rings made of different metals for your projects.

Advantages of using anodized aluminum rings

Anodized aluminum rings come highly recommended. Here are some reasons why:

- Anodized aluminum is the most inexpensive metal to work with. While standard aluminum alloy rings might be even cheaper, anodized aluminum will not react and fade over time.
- It is better to use anodized aluminum instead of gold and sterling silver because you can choose from different colors, and therefore your projects can be easily customized.
- Stainless steel rings are very difficult to open and close. Even titanium rings are quite difficult to open and close. This is not the case for anodized aluminum.

Choose the Right Gauge

The best gauge size that a beginner should start with is 18 gauge. Remember, gauge affects the size and width of the jewelry you make. If you use 14 gauge rings for your project it will have a very chunky effect. It is suitable for making chunky bracelets and necklaces. If 16 gauge rings are used, the project will be sleeker than the 14 gauge projects.

Of course, you have the freedom to choose whichever gauge you want, but many believe it is ideal to work with 18 gauge. Here are a few benefits of using 18 gauge:

- It is quite sturdy.
- This gauge is fairly easy to work with.
- It does not warp easily.

You can use 20-gauge if you are making earrings or something more petite. It is light and has a dainty appearance.

Buy the Right Kind of Rings

You should buy only saw-cut jump rings for making jewelry. The reason is that machine-cut jump rings have angles on them, and so they don't close flush. That said, if you are only practicing, machine-cut will work fine; but, when making real, quality jewelry saw-cut jump rings are essential.

Tip:

When talking to the supplier about jump rings, always make sure to clarify whether they are talking about ID or OD.

Tools

If you are making your own jump rings you will need a few more tools (a wire, a mandrel, calipers, and a flush cutter) than if you buy ready-made jump rings. If you buy your jump rings, the only additional tools you need to start making chain maille are: two pairs of pliers.

A large variety of pliers are available in the market. Some of them are very expensive while others do not cost much. Their prices may vary between $5 and $50 or more.

As you will need to have two pairs of pliers for making chain maille and there are many different varieties to choose from. That said, do not buy pliers that have saw tooth or a rough interior because you will damage your rings with them. Always make sure that you buy pliers that have a smooth interior. Here are a few varieties you can choose from:

A chain nose pliers

It has a flat inside jaw. It is very sharp at the end. It is useful when you are using rings that have a smaller gauge.

Flat nose pliers

These pliers are different from the chain nose plier because it has a wide jaw and a wider tip. It is useful for larger gauge jump rings because when you use larger gauge rings you need more gripping area.

Bent nose pliers

Bent nose pliers have, you guessed it, a bent shape at the end and their tips are very fine. If you want to have a nice tight grip you can grip a ring with its elbow.

Tips:

- Never get the pliers with a saw tooth interior, or even a rough interior, this might rough up the surface of the jump rings.
- You can buy Tool Magic and coat the jaws and tips of the pliers so that the rings do not get damaged by their sharp surfaces or tips.

Suppliers

You can get anodized aluminum rings from the following suppliers:

1. Jump Ring Suppliers for Making Chainmaille Jewelry

http://www.bluebuddhaboutique.com/blog/2016/07/jump-ring-suppliers-for-making-chainmaille-jewelry/

2. Chainmail Rings and Supplies - West Coast Chainmail

www.chainmaildude.com › store › jump-rings-for-chainmail

3. Weave Got Maille

https://weavegotmaille.com/chainmaille-kits/

4. Aussie Maille

https://www.aussiemaille.com › anodized-aluminum-jump-rings

5. Metal Designz

https://www.metaldesignz.com › Jump Rings

CHAPTER 3: EUROPEAN 4 IN 1

In this pattern four jump rings are connected to one jump ring. Series of columns and rows are connected with one jump ring. The European 4 in 1 chain maille technique forms the foundation for medieval armor. You can utilize it for making jewelry and many other things, too.

This is the most popular weaves in chain maille. Many other patterns are based on it. When you use this design one flat strip is formed in which all the rings go through four rings, except the rings on the edge. You can use this weave to make sheets or wider strips.

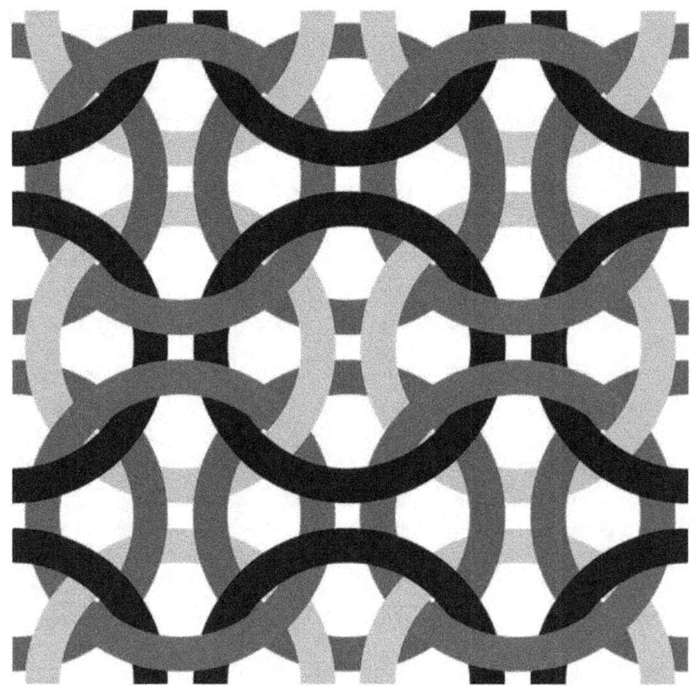

Things required

Rings: 18 gauge, ID 4mm

Two pairs of pliers

Instructions

Step 1

Open some of the jump rings. Close some of the jump rings. Take one jump ring that you have opened and put four closed ones into it. Close the open jump ring.

Step 2

Put all the rings in a flat position. The closed jump ring must be in the center and it should be tilted upwards on your side. The other four outer rings should be tilted downwards on your side.

This forms the 4 in 1 pattern in which there is one connector jump ring in the center and four rings on the outer side. The four rings make the rows and columns.

Step 3

In order to add another column, open one jump ring. Then put two closes rings into it.

Step 4

Join the opened jump ring with the two jump rings that are in column number two. You should add columns like this until you reach the width that you want for the design that you have chosen.

Step 5

In order to begin another row, take one open ring and put two closed rings into it. Join the open ring to the first two rings in the second row.

Step 6

If you want to add more rings to the row, put one closed ring into one open ring and join it to the second and third jump rings in row two and the second ring that is there in row three.

Step 7

Keep adding the rows until the desired length is achieved.

Speed Weaving

There is one more way of weaving the 4 in 1 pattern. It is known as speed weaving. It is a little faster than the previous method.

Step 1

You should start making the pattern in a similar way as you did earlier. Take one opened jump ring and put four closed jump rings into it. Then close the open ring.

Step 2

Lay the rings in such a way that there are two-two rings on either side of the connecting jump ring.

Step 3

Then take one opened ring and put two closed rings into it.

Step 4

Join this open ring to two of the closed rings that are at one of the ends of the previous link that you have made.

Keep repeating this pattern and create one chain, which is sufficiently long for the item you are planning to make.

Step 5

Lay the rings in such a manner that the connecting rings in the center are tilted upwards on your side. The outer rings should be tilted downwards on your side.

Step 6

Make one more similar chain. This will be for the next section.

Step 7

Lay both the chains side by side. In each chain, the ring in the center should be tilted upwards on your side and the outer rings should be tilted downwards on your side like before.

Step 8

Take one opened jump ring and join the first two rings that are there in row two, and the first two rings that are in row three.

Step 9

Then take another opened jump ring and join the second and third jump rings from row two and the second and third jump rings, from row three, together.

Step 10

In this same way, continue using the open rings to join both the chains together.

If you keep the center connector rings tilted upwards on your side, the chain maille fabric will remain relatively rectangular. The sides will continue to retain their shape. For belts and bracelets, this orientation is best.

But the fabric's drape will change if the fabric is turned ninety degrees. The sides will collapse inwards on themselves. They will taper towards the bottom. For shirts, this orientation is correct because the fabric follows the body's contours.

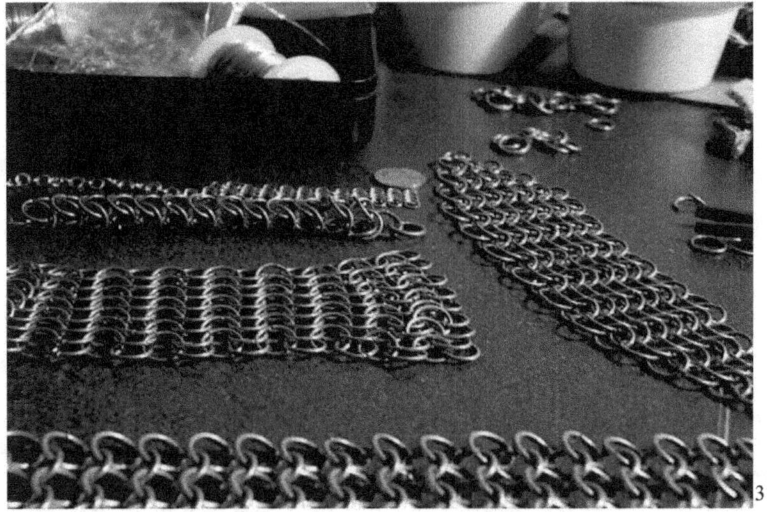

[3] NiaSkywalk. (2009, July 1). Chain Maille. Retrieved from

CHAPTER 4: EUROPEAN 6 IN 1

This weave is a simple progression of the European 4 in 1. In this, all the rings pass through six rings and create a more dense fabric compared to the 4 in 1 version.

If you use the same sized rings and make something with the 4 in 1 and 6 in 1 techniques you will find that density is the main difference between the two. It is easier to make 4 in 1 and that technique is certainly very suitable for some projects. But in case you want a denser weave, you should use 6 in 1.

Things required

Rings: 18 gauge, ID 5 mm

Two pairs of pliers

Instructions

Step 1

If you are making a bracelet using the European 6 in 1 technique, first you should begin by making the width.

Close six rings and open one ring. Put the six rings into the opened ring. Then close this ring and place the four rings one on top of the other and let two remain to one side. This is the first 6 in 1 that you have made.

Step 2

Open one ring and put three of the last rings into it. Then add three more rings to it and close it.

Step 3

Repeat Step 2.

Step 4

Now you will have three privileged rings. Each privileged ring will have six rings going through them. You can name them the 'boss rings.'

Step 5

Now you should make the length of the bracelet.

Go back to the first 6 in 1 piece. Open one ring and pass it through the four bottom rings. You should take it below a boss ring. Remember to take it from the right to the left.

Step 6

Then add two closed rings to the opened ring. Working in this way, you should have six rings in one ring. Close the opened ring.

Note:

While making some tight jewelry you may have to lift the piece so that you can close the open rings correctly. After doing so you can arrange the item and just pat it; otherwise, you can move all the rings into their original positions, if necessary.

Step 7

Then open another ring and pass it below the second boss ring. Take it through the five rings (two from the right, plus three from the left).

Step 8

Add one ring to it so that there are six rings in one ring. Then close the open ring.

Step 9

After that, move to the following boss ring. Repeat Step 7 and Step 8.

Note:

If you want to make fine jewelry, use rings that have nice cuts. In addition to this, you should see to it that after closing the rings that there are no gaps in between. It is advisable to pass one fine plier on the edges after you close the ring. You should do so on both sides using a rotating motion. If you do not close and brush the rings' beaks with pliers there might be a chance they could scratch your skin.

However, only use a pair of fine pliers. Any other pliers may damage the rings.

So, as a reminder, you should be patient and close each ring properly. This will give strength and beauty to your jewelry.

CHAPTER 5: THE HALF PERSIAN 3 IN 1

The Half Persian 3 in 1 weave is very useful for making bracelets, key chains, necklaces, among other things. It requires only one size of jump ring.

The cross-section of this weave is chevron-shaped so it has two faces.

Things required

Rings with minimum 4 aspect ratio

Two pairs of pliers

For making one loose sheet

Wire: 1.68 millimeter

Inner Dimension: 8.30 millimeter

For a tight sheet

Wire: 1.52 millimeter

Inner Dimension: 6.25 millimeter

Instructions

Pattern facing left

Step 1

Take one open ring and put two closed rings into it. Close the open ring. Lay the rings in such a way that they lay halfway, one above the other, from the left to the right.

We can name the jump ring that has two rings inside it 'little boss.' We can call the other two rings the 'underlings.'

Step 2

Now you should pass one open ring through the rings we've named the underlings. While doing so, you should take it above the little boss ring.

Step 3

Put one closed ring into it so that you have three rings in one ring. Then close the ring. This is the boss ring.

Make sure that the underling that you have just added is below the others.

Step 4

Put one closed ring in an open ring. Pass it through the previous two underlings. Then close the ring.

Step 5

Arrange the rings in such a way that the boss rings lie above the boss rings, and the underlings lie one under the other underling. This is the general rule for this technique.

Repeat the above steps to complete the chain or sheet with this pattern.

This model has two faces. In a case wherein you make one tight piece, the item will bend with just the left face.

Pattern facing right

Step 1

Take one open ring and put two closed rings into it. Close the open ring and place the rings in such a manner that the underlings lay halfway, one above the other from the left side to the right side.

Step 2

Put one closed ring into an open ring. Pass it through the underling rings. Then close the ring and lay them according to the rule that has been stated earlier.

Repeat the steps until you get to your desired length and width of the chain or sheet.

Finishing touch

If there are any rebel rings in the starting part of the chain or sheet, you can remove them and put in one smaller ring to attach the clasp (if you are planning to make a necklace or bracelet). In this way, you can form one nice pattern as well as a bending face.

CHAPTER 6: HALF PERSIAN 4 IN 1

Half Persian 4 in 1 is very useful for making bracelets, necklaces, anklets, straps for purses, and garments.

The cross-section of this chain is rectangular in shape. It is a progression of the Half Persian 3 in 1.

Here you can learn how to do the Half Persian 4 in 1 using a template to stabilize the rings while developing the pattern.

Method 1 - Using a Maille Card

Things required

Maille card

Rings: 18 gauge, ID 5 mm

Two pairs of pliers

Instructions

Step 1

Put some rings on the maille card. If you do not have a maille card you can take any other card and punch some holes on its edges. Place the rings in such a manner that one side of the first ring is in the first slit and the other side of the ring is in the third slit.

One side of the second ring should be in the second slit, that means the slit that lies in the middle of the first ring. The other side of the ring should be in the fourth slit.

Place the third ring above the second ring in the third slit. The other side of the ring should be in the fifth slit.

Similarly, place the fourth ring above the third ring in the fourth slit. The other side of the fourth ring should be in the sixth slit.

In this way, the rings lie halfway above each other.

The area enclosed by the rings when they intersect each other is known as an 'eye.'

Step 2

To make the half Persian pattern you have to take one open ring through an eye, then around an eye, and again through another eye. After passing the ring in this way you can close it neatly with the help of pliers.

Step 3

Put one more closed ring on the card. Pass one open ring through one eye, around one eye, and again through another eye. Close the ring.

Stabilize your work and remove the chain from the card.

Step 4

Put one open ring through the last ring, around an eye, and again through another eye. Put one closed ring into the open ring to create a new eye and then close it.

Repeat this step until you reach the desired length. To finish it, put one open ring through one eye, around one eye, and again through another eye and close the ring. Do not add a closed ring to create another eye.

Method 2 - Using Tape

Things required

Rings: 18 gauge, ID 5mm

Scotch tape, masking tape, sticker, duct tape, or anything that has an adhesive such as a shipping label

Pliers (long nose)

Pliers (round nose)

Step 1

Cut one broad strip of a shipping label or tape. Stick the rings one by one on one edge of the adhesive side of the label. The rings should overlap one another. Put as many rings as the label can hold.

Step 2

Then fold the label or tape into half in such a way that the rings are sandwiched in the middle of the fold. Press lightly.

Step 3

Take one opened ring and pass it through one eye, around one eye, and again through one eye of the rings. Close the ends of the ring using two pairs of pliers. Pass another opened ring through the next eye in a similar manner.

Repeat this step again and again until you finish putting opened rings in all the eyes.

Then remove the chain from the shipping label or tape.

Method 3

Things required

Anodized aluminum rings of two different colors yellow and white: 18 gauge, ID 5mm

Two pairs of pliers

Instructions

Step 1

Put two closed white rings in one open yellow ring. Then close the open ring.

Step 2

Place the two white rings in such a way that one of them is under the other one and the second ring is facing right.

Step 3

You can see that an eye is formed between the two white rings. Take another yellow ring and pass it through this eye. While doing so make sure that it goes above the previous yellow ring.

Note:

In the beginning the chain is not set properly; so, you should not move it around too much, otherwise the shape may go awry.

Step 4

Now an eye will be formed by the yellow jump rings. Take a white open ring and pass it through this eye. While doing this see to it that the ring goes under the previous white ring.

Step 5

If you are not using a variety of colors you have to take note of which eye has just been formed. But when you are using colors you can see that the eye colors are alternating between white rings, and next time, yellow rings.

So now there will be one white eye. Take one yellow ring and pass it through this eye. Remember that it should move above the last yellow ring, facing left.

Step 6

You can see that all the yellow color rings face left and all the white rings face right. This is exactly the design that you are striving to create.

In this design, you change the way of moving the rings in an alternating fashion. Previously, while moving one ring through an eye you took it above the last ring while now you will take it *under* the last ring.

You can continue to repeat the steps until you reach the desired length for your project.

Method 4

Things required

Anodized aluminum rings of 2 different colors yellow and white: 18 gauge, ID 5mm

Two pairs of pliers

Instructions

Step 1

Make two sets of rings. One group should contain white closed rings and the other should have yellow opened rings.

Step 2

Arrange three closed white rings so that they overlap each other, lying halfway with one below the other, and facing towards the right.

Step 3

Then pass a yellow ring through one eye that has been formed in the previous step. The ring should go under the rings from the right to the left side.

You might be familiar with the tricky ways in which the rings move around. With this in mind, it may be easier for you to put three white rings in one yellow ring and arrange the rings later. You can place the rings in such a manner that the three white rings overlap each other halfway and the yellow ring goes through one eye, then under the white rings from the right to the left side and finally coming up from the last ring.

Step 4

Then pass one open yellow ring through the first eye that is formed by white rings. Take the ring above the previous yellow ring, moving from the left to the right. When the yellow ring is below the last one (white color ring) put one more closed ring in it and close the ring. This white closed jump ring will get fitted below.

Repeat this procedure through the second white eye, then the third white eye. Continue doing so until you reach the desired length.

CHAPTER 7: JAPANESE 12 IN 2

This weave forms an exquisite shape like a flower. The chain is made with two different sizes of rings. The small ones have to be sufficiently large to hold two large rings and the large rings should be in a position to hold twelve small rings.

The Japanese 12 in 2 weave is suitable for making pendants, bracelets, and watches. There are several ways of making this pattern. You can either start by keeping the smaller-sized rings open and the larger-sized rings closed or the reverse of that. Otherwise, you can use a free-style, which means you can open and close a ring whenever you use it.

If you use small open rings and weave them through the larger ones, sometimes they become deformed when they are closed because of the opposition they face from the rings inside them. Therefore, it is preferable to pass larger-sized open jump rings carefully through the closed smaller rings.

Thing required

14 bright aluminum jump rings: 18 gauge, 4.8 millimeter ID

24 purple colored anodized aluminum jump rings 20-gauge, 3.2 millimeter ID

Two pairs of pliers

Instructions

Step 1

Open one large-sized jump ring. Put eight closed small-sized jump rings into it. Close the larger ring. Pass another large open jump ring through on this same route. Close the second large jump ring.

Step 2

Put four of the small open rings in the large-sized rings from the first step. Close the small rings. Now there should be a total of 12 small-sized rings in the two larger ones.

Step 3

Put one new large-sized ring through two small-sized rings from Step 1 and Step 2. Put four closed smaller rings into it before closing it. Weave another large open jump ring. Ensure that it passes through all of the six small rings during this step. Then close this second large-sized jump ring.

Step 4

Take another opened large size jump ring. Pass it through two small rings from the center (Step 1 and Step 2). Also pass it through the two small jump rings, which you added during the previous move. After that, put two more small closed jump rings and then close the large-sized ring. Pass another large-sized ring through this same route and close the ring.

Step 5

You should repeat the fourth step three times. When your work progresses one flower pattern will emerge.

Step 6

Weave one open large-sized ring through the six small rings that are left hanging. They are two from the center (Step 1 and Step 2), two from the third step, and two from repeating the fourth for the third time. After putting it through these rings, close it. Weave one more open large-sized ring through this same route and close the ring.

With this, your Japanese 12 in 2 weave is complete.

CHAPTER 8: SPIRAL AND DOUBLE SPIRAL

Spiral

This pattern is suitable for bracelets and necklaces.

Things required

Rings: 18 gauge, ID 4mm

Two pairs of pliers

Instructions

Step 1

Open some rings and keep them ready for use. Take one closed ring and put it into one open ring. Close it with the help of pliers.

Step 2

Hold the two rings in such a way that they overlap each other and there is a small gap where they intersect.

Step 3

Take one open ring and put it in the gap. Take it under the previous ring and around the present ring. Then close it.

Step 4

Hold the chain in such a manner that the rings overlap each other and you can see a gap between the previous and the present ring where they intersect.

Repeat the steps given above until you get the length that you want for the object you are making. If you twist the chain, you can see that it forms a spiral.

Double Spiral

Things required

Rings: 18 gauge, ID 4mm

Two pairs of pliers

Instructions

Step 1

In order to get ready to make the pattern, open 20 rings and keep two closed rings.

Take one open ring and put the two closed rings into it. Close the open ring.

Step 2

Hold the two closed rings and put one open ring into it. Then close the ring.

Step 3

Hold the four rings in such a manner that two rings are on one side and the other two rings are on the other side and a tiny eye is formed where they intersect each other. Take one open ring and put it through that tiny eye and close it.

Step 4

Take one open ring and put it through the same spot between the four rings where you put the previous ring. Close it. Take the single ring that you previously put through the eye and hold it beside the ring that you have just closed.

So, if you lay the rings there will be sets of two-two rings overlapping each other.

Step 5

If you hold the previous four rings together you will see that a tiny eye is formed at the place where they intersect. Take one open ring and put it through that tiny eye and close it.

Take another ring and put it through the same spot between the four rings where you put the previous ring.

As you keep repeating the above steps and the double spiral chain grows, it will become easier for you to see the gap or eye between the previous four rings through which you have to put the next open ring.

To finish the chain you can add a smaller ring maybe an 18 gauge, 3/16 inch at the end. Put this ring through the small gap or eye between the previous four rings just as if you were continuing the pattern and close it. This will give a tapered-off effect to the chain. After that, you can attach a clasp or end cap according to the item you are making.

CHAPTER 9: THE BYZANTINE PATTERN

The Byzantine weave is also known as the 'Birdcage.' Although it looks complicated, it is quite easy to make. It is suitable for making bracelets and can be used for making pendants and earrings as well.

If you want to pleasantly surprise your friends, give make and give them a Byzantine chain maille bracelet as a gift. They will surely be impressed by its flexibility and intricate appearance.

This chain is actually made by creating several units of the Box Chain 4 in 1 pattern and there are connector rings that separate them.

Things required

Two sets of two different color rings: 1/4 inch, 16 gauge, blue and black color rings

Instructions

Step 1

Start by making a two-two-two chain. This means that you put four black rings into two blue rings. Then spread them out in such a manner that the two blue rings are in the center and there are two-two black rings on either side of the blue ring.

In order to make it clear as to which side you are working on, put one different color ring of a larger size at one end.

Step 2

Open one blue ring to get ready for the next step.

Use alternate colors so that blue rings will go through black rings and black rings will go through blue rings.

Flip the two black rings that you have put in the two-two-two chain to a backwards position. Position them in such a way that they come out at the center between the previous two blue rings. Then put the open blue ring into them and close the ring. This is actually a single unit of the box chain pattern.

Step 3

Open two more blue rings and put them in through the two black rings at the same spot as the previous blue ring and close them. So you will have three blue rings together at one spot.

Step 4

Open two black rings and put them through the three blue rings that you just added and close them.

Step 5

Open two blue rings and put them through the two black rings that you just added and close them.

Step 6

Open one black ring and get it ready for the next step. Flip the two blue rings backwards. Position them in such a way that they come out at the center between the previous two black rings. Then put the open black ring into them and close the ring. Now you have made two units of the box chain pattern.

Step 7

Open two more black rings and put them in through the two blue rings at the same spot as the previous black ring and close them. So you will have three black rings together at one spot.

Step 8

Open two blue rings and put them through the three black rings that you just added and close them.

Step 9

Open two black rings and put them through the two blue rings that you just added and close them.

Repeat from Step 2 onwards and continue weaving until you reach the desired length of the object that you are making.

CHAPTER 10: DRAGON SCALE DESIGN

Although the Dragon Scale design is a complicated weave in chain maille it is also an intricate and beautiful weave nonetheless. You may need to spend some more time and work with more patience, but rest assured that the ultimate result will be fabulous.

This weave is flexible and impressive. It is related to the basic European 4 in 1 design. It is a unique chain maille pattern because two different sized rings are used in it and the small ones fit into the bigger ones. You can make a stunning necklace or an intricate bracelet for your friends and show off your skills.

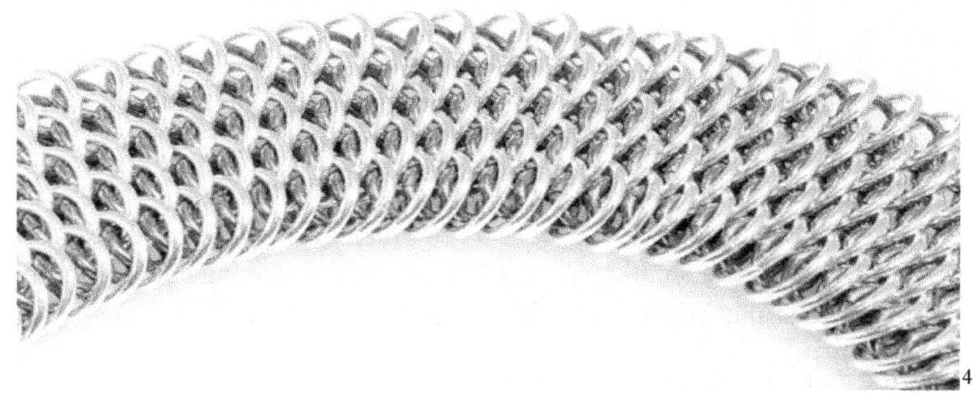

Things required

Two different colors and sizes of rings

Larger white color rings: 18 gauge, ID 15 inch

Smaller black color rings: 20 gauge, ID 9 inch

Two pairs of pliers

Instructions

Step 1

If you are making a bracelet with this weave, first you have to establish the width and then work down the length.

Open some of the smaller rings and close the larger rings properly. As you will need some open smaller rings and some closed larger rings for this step.

---

[4] The ChainMaille Lady. (2011, March 4). Dragonscale bracelet sterling silver & pink niobium. Retrieved from

https://www.flickr.com/photos/thechainmaillelady/5560087101/in/pool---chainmail_jewelery_and_armor--/

In this design, you can start with four large rings and three small rings.

Put one small and one large ring together, alternating, to make a chain.

Step 2

Close three larger rings and get them ready for this step. In this step, you are going to put the larger rings on the smaller ones.

Hold one larger ring on a smaller ring. Take one open larger ring and take it through the smaller ring and close it. In this way, the loose larger ring will be captured in place on top of the smaller ring.

Step 3

In this you step, you will capture another loose larger ring. Hold one closed larger ring on top of a smaller ring. Take one open larger ring and take it through the previous smaller ring and the smaller ring that is under the new loose ring, and close it.

In this way, both the previous and the present loose larger rings will be captured and will remain in the right place.

Step 4

Place one closed larger ring on the next smaller ring. Take one open larger ring and pass it through the previous smaller ring and the smaller ring that is under the loose larger ring and close it.

Take one open larger ring and put it through the last smaller ring.

Step 5

Lay the piece in such a way that you have three rows of rings. The first row consists of four larger rings. The second row consists of three larger rings. The third row consists of four larger rings. So the rows will consist of alternating rings of four and three.

The larger ones will be stacked in one direction and the smaller ones will be stacked in another direction and you will have a criss-cross pattern on the edge of the piece.

Step 6

Take one open smaller ring and put it through the top larger ring and capture the larger ring from the row before and close it.

Open one smaller ring and put it in from the top, take it in the middle of one larger ring and take it out from the middle of the next larger ring from the row before and close it.

Then take another open smaller ring and put it in from the top in the middle of one larger ring and take it out from the next larger ring from the row before and close it.

Once again put one open smaller ring from the top through the larger ring from the row before and close it.

In this way, you will have a new row of four smaller rings sitting inside the larger rings.

Step 7

You will continue working in alternating rows of three rings and four rings.

Take one open larger ring and put it through two smaller rings from the previous row and close it.

Do the same for all the smaller rings in the row.

This row will now have three large rings.

Repeat Step 6 and Step 7 until you reach the desired length of the piece.

Step 8

Start tapering with a row of three larger rings. Continue doing Step 6 and Step 7, but use only two larger rings in the next sequence and finally use just one larger ring in the last row.

You can attach whatever kind of end caps or findings you like to this final larger ring.

CHAPTER 11: MAKE COLORFUL PROJECTS AND USE RINGS OF DIFFERENT SIZES

Make a Colorful Spiral 4 in 1 Weave

A spiral weave is a simple chain maille weave in which the chain forms a spiral when it is twisted in one direction. If it is twisted forwards it does not form a spiral; only if it is twisted backwards will it spiral. After that spiral, if you put clasps at the ends it remains in that shape.

Things required

Red, blue and golden rings: 18 gauge, ID 4mm

Two pairs of pliers

Instructions

Step 1

To start, put one red ring on a twine and add one golden ring to it. Hold them in such a manner that the two rings overlap and the golden ring is on top of the red ring and an eye is formed where they intersect.

Step 2

Open one blue ring and put it in through that eye or gap that is formed at the intersection of the red and golden rings and close it.

Step 3

Hold the rings in such a way that the blue ring lies on top of the golden ring. Again, one eye will be formed at the place where the two rings intersect.

Step 4

Open one red ring and put it through the eye that is formed between the blue and golden rings and close it.

Step 5

Hold the blue and red rings in such a manner that the red ring lies above the blue ring and one eye is formed at the spot where the two rings intersect.

Step 6

Open one golden ring and put it through the eye and close it.

Repeat the steps using red, golden, and then blue--one after the other.

After you reach the desired length, twist the chain backwards and form a spiral. Then put clasps or end caps on when it is still in that spiral position, so that it remains as a spiral chain. This is the way to make a colorful chain maille item.

Similarly, you can use rings of different colors in your weaves and make any chain maille pattern more or less colorful, according to your preference.

Variations of European 4 in 1 Using Different Sized Rings

Here are some of the variations that can be made in the European 4 in 1 weave, simply by modifying the ring sizes.

Things required

Rings: 16 gauge, 3/16 inch ID

Rings: 18 gauge, 3/16 inch ID

Rings: 16 gauge, 1/4 inch ID

Two pairs of pliers

Instructions

Step 1

In order to prepare for the first step, open some rings and close some rings. Keep two closed rings with each open ring.

Put two closed rings in one open ring.

Step 2

Spread the two rings out like a butterfly's wings on the connecting ring. Take one open ring and pass it through the two rings in such a manner that the ring enters the first ring from below and enters the second ring from above.

Then add two closed rings to this open ring and close it.

Repeat the steps to make small sample pieces with all the three different sizes of rings represented.

Rings with the same gauge, but a different ID

- You will see that the 16 gauge, 3/16 inch rings and 16 gauge, 1/4 inch rings have the same wire size but their inner diameters are different. The variance between their inner diameters makes a big difference in the appearance of the weave.
- The ring that has a 3/16 inch ID makes a more tight and dense weave.
- The weave made with the rings that have 1/4 inch diameter has more movement and stretch. This weave is suitable for making costume pieces or adding weave to shirts or dresses.

Rings with a different gauge, but the same ID

A weave done with 16 gauge rings is tighter, while a weave made with 18 gauge rings is airier. So, by reducing the width of the wire the weave can be more spacious and loose compared to the thicker wire.

Adding Stretchy Rings to the Weaves

There are many different ways in which you can use Rubber O-Rings in chain maille. There are different sizes of rings that can be used, for example, 7.25 mm, 10 mm, and 12 mm. These rings can be used to make your with chain maille a bit more stretchy and flexible. You can use these rings with any chain maille weave and make stretchable bracelets, too.

European 4 in 1 Stretchy Chain Maille

European 4 in 1 is one of the basic weaves of chain maille. It is considered to be a beginner's weave. Many other weaves are based on it. In order to make a stretchy version of this weave you can use EPDM rings, which are actually rubber rings. These rings are available in three sizes. They are:

- 16 gauge AWG 1.2 mm diameter wire and 3/16 inch or 4.76 mm ID

To weave an eight-inch or 20 cm long bracelet you need 39 metal rings and 78 EPDM rings.

- 14 gauge AWG 1.6 mm diameter wire and 1/4 inch or 6.35 mm ID

To weave an eight-inch or 20 cm long bracelet you need 31 metal rings and 62 EPDM rings.

- 14 gauge AWG 1.6 mm diameter wire and 5/16 inch or 7.94 mm ID

To weave an eight-inch or 20 cm long bracelet you need 22 metal rings and 44 EPDM rings.

The 16 gauge weave has a good elasticity while the other two are less stretchable compared to it. This weave is good for bracelets and also for making a choker. While for bracelets you can perform this weave without adding clasps. However, you must put clasps on when you make a choker, as this piece of jewelry is not meant to go over your head.

Things required

A twist tie, a piece of wire, or a paper-clip

2 pairs of smooth jawed pliers

Instructions

Step 1

Open one metal ring and put two EPDM rings into it. Take the twist tie and put it through the metal ring and twist it. This will give you a handle to hold on to when you start the chain.

Step 2

Spread out the two EPDM rings so that the metal ring's head is on top of them. Then take one open metal ring and put it into the first and second EPDM rings. Add two more EPDM rings and close the metal ring.

Repeat this step until you have used all the rings. In this way, you will have a strip, which has three rows.

If you are making a bracelet, go back to the beginning part and remove the twist tie. Then you have to put the two ends together; so, turn it into a circle and see that the last rings match the design. Open the first metal ring and put the last two EPDM rings into it and close it. In this way, you can complete the round bracelet.

Expanding a Stretchy Bracelet

You now have a bracelet with three rows of rings. If you want to make it broader you can easily follow these steps.

Expand a bracelet by using metal rings

Step 1

Take the strip of three rows and hold two EPDM rings that are already on one corner of the bracelet in such a way that they overlap and one eye is formed where they intersect.

Step 2

Open one metal ring and put it through that eye or gap at the spot where the two EPDM rings intersect and then close it.

Step 3

Take another open metal ring and put it through the next EPDM ring and the previous EPDM ring through which you have already put one metal ring. Close the ring.

Repeat these steps for all the rings until you have a new row of metal rings on the side of the strip.

After that, repeat the steps on the other side of the strip until you have a new row of metal rings on the other side, too.

Remember that the metal rings in the side rows should be positioned in the same way as the metal rings in the middle row. For example, if the metal rings in the center are sitting on top, then the side rings should also be on top. If the metal rings in the center are sitting underneath, then the side rings should also be underneath.

After you complete these steps you will have a strip that has five rows. Three rows are made with metal rings and two rows are made with EPDM rings.

Expand a bracelet by using rubber rings

Step 1

Go to the beginning part of the strip. Take one open metal ring and put it into the first EPDM ring on the right, add one more EPDM ring and close the ring.

Step 2

Hold the new EPDM ring in position beside the previous EPDM ring in such a way that the head of the metal ring is on top of both of them.

Step 3

Take one open metal ring and put it through the EPDM ring on the right, the EPDM ring on the left, and the EPDM ring on the top. Then add one new EPDM ring to it and close it.

Repeat the steps until there are two new rows of rings on the side. After you complete these steps there will be two rows of metal rings and three rows of EPDM rings. So altogether there will be five rows in the strip.

While doing the steps remember to check that the position of the new EPDM rings matches the position of the earlier EPDM rings.

CHAPTER 12: CHARTS AND RESOURCES

Here are a few extremely helpful tables that will eliminate a lot of math and will allow you to know the gauge wire diameter (inner & outer) as well as aspect ratio if you don't have enough information to complete the aspect ratio equation. These charts are especially useful if you know the wire gauge, but don't have calipers with you. Moreover, you can also learn the ring sizes for both sterling silver and anodized aluminum.

AWG to SWG Wire Gauge Conversion Chart [5]

Wire Gauge	Precious Metal (AWG)	Base Metal (SWG)
24		0.02" 0.5 mm
22		0.025" 0.6 mm
21	0.029" 0.724 mm	
20	0.032" 0.8 mm	0.032" 0.8 mm
19	0.036" 0.912 mm	
18	0.04" 1.024 mm	0.048" 1.2 mm
17	0.045" 1.15 mm	
16	0.051" 1.291 mm	0.062" 1.6 mm
14	0.064" 1.63 mm	0.08" 2.0 mm

---

[5] What do your ring names mean. Retrieved from

https://www.bluebuddhaboutique.com/b3/faq/ringsize/B3-ring-names

13	--	--
12	0.081" 2.025 mm	0.104" 2.64 mm
11	--	--
10	0.102" 2.588 mm	0.128" 3.25 mm

Note:

Some examples of precious metals are sterling silver, gold-fill, titanium, and niobium.

Base metals refer to the metals that corrode or oxidize easily. Some examples of base metals are brass, copper, bronze, enameled copper, stainless steel, and aluminum.

Wire Gauge Conversion Chart [6]

Sizes listed are AWG (American Wire Gauge)

Wire Gauge	Inches	Millimeters
6	0.162	4.11
8	0.129	3.27
9	0.114	2.91
10	0.102	2.56
12	0.081	2.05
14	0.064	1.63
15	0.057	1.45

---

[6] Measurements, gauges & jewelry terms. Retrieved from

http://www.rings-things.com/Learn/Wire-Chart/

16	0.051	1.30
17	0.045	1.14
18	0.040	1.02
19	0.036	0.914
20	0.032	0.813
21	0.029	0.737
22	0.025	0.635
24	0.020	0.508
25	0.018	0.455
26	0.016	0.406
28	0.013	0.320
30	0.010	0.254
32	0.008	0.203

Note: Remember that as the gauge increases the thickness decreases. So a larger gauge wire is thinner than a wire that has a lower gauge number.

Wire Gauge Table [7]

Inside Diameter (ID)

Listed ID does not include springback - this is specific to each material and listed in the catalog

---

[7] Wire gauges and ring sizes. Retrieved from

https://theringlord.com/cart/shopcontent.asp?type=WireGauge

Ring Measurement Chart		1/16"	5/64"	3/32"	7/64"	1/8"	9/64"	5/32"	11/64"	3/16"	7/32"	1/4"	9/32"	5/16"	3/8"	7/16"	1/2"
		.0625"	.0781"	.0938"	.1094"	.125"	.1406"	.1563"	.1719"	.1875"	.2188"	.25"	.0281"	.3125"	.375"	.4375"	.50"
		1.6 mm	2.0 mm	2.4 mm	2.8 mm	3.2 mm	3.6 mm	4.0 mm	4.4 mm	4.8 mm	5.6 mm	6.4 mm	7.1 mm	7.9 mm	9.5 mm	11.1 mm	12.7 mm
Wire Thickness (It may vary for each material - see the catalog for exact numbers)	24 g (AWG) 0.02" 0.5 mm	3.2	4.0	4.8	5.6	6.4											
	22 g (AWG) 0.025"		3.3	4.0	4.6	5.3	6.0	6.6									

	0.6 mm														
	20 g (AWG) 0.032" 0.8 mm			3.0	3.5	4.0	4.5	5.0	5.5	6.0					
	19g (SWG) 0.04" 1.0 mm					3.2	3.6	4.0	4.4	4.8	5.6	6.4	7.1	7.9	
	18g (SWG) 0.048" 1.2 mm					2.6	3.0	3.3	3.6	4.0	4.6	5.4	6.0	6.6	7.9

16g (SWG) 0.062" 1.6 mm									3.0	3.5	4.0	4.5	5.0	6.0	6.9	
14g (SWG) 0.08" 2.0 mm											3.2	3.6	4.0	4.8	5.6	6.4
12g (SWG) 0.1" 2.5 mm													3.2	3.8	4.4	5.1

This table shows the data for the rings in both AWG and SWG gauge systems. However, the actual ring may be slightly bigger because of springback. Rings made of harder materials such as stainless steel may be bigger than those made with softer materials.

So, you should always note the actual wire size, ID, and AR mentioned on the rings when buying them. This is very important when you want to make a weave that is highly dependent on the aspect ratio; for example, if you are making some tight weave this will be very important.

Easy Calculations

Use an AR calculator

If you want to avoid doing the math and want to know the AR of jump rings directly, you can use various AR calculators that are available online.

For example, you can use the Simple Aspect Ratio Calculator available at Blue Buddha Boutique.

Found at: https://www.bluebuddhaboutique.com/b3/ring_sizes/aspect_ratio

You just have to enter the ring's inner diameter and then enter the wire's diameter.

Remember to use the same system of measurement while entering both the ring's inner diameter and the wire's thickness. In case you know only the gauge of the wire, convert it into millimeters or inches before entering it in the calculator.

Moreover, various suppliers make use of different systems of measuring the thickness of the wire so you should get all the exact numbers and measurements from the supplier directly.

After you enter the two values into the calculator the AR will be visible.

You can repeat the process for other sizes of rings, entering the new ID and WD of the other rings and calculating the AR for all of them one by one.

Note:

I do not own any of the above calculators or websites; they are made and/or owned by other people.

Know the RPI

Rings per inch (RPI) helps you to know the number of rings that are used for making one inch of the particular item. Using this measurement, you can easily find out how many jump rings you will need for the entire length of the item that you are planning to make. In cases wherein you are making something bigger, such as a sheet that covers a larger surface area, then you can use the RPI that tells rings used per square inch.

CONCLUSION

Here are a few useful tips for beginners:

1. Do not make your own rings

When you make your first maille project, do not waste your time in making the hundreds of jump rings that you will need. There are plenty of sources where you can get readymade jump rings that are good enough for any project. Buy some jump rings and enjoy the fun of linking the rings and making patterns of your choice.

2. Buy anodized aluminum rings

Use anodized aluminum rings for your initial projects because they are not very expensive and you can easily use them for practice. Another reason to use these rings, is that they are available in various colors so you can make colorful projects already at the beginning of your learning and gain immediate satisfaction and enjoyment.

3. Be careful about the ring's ID

When you are buying rings for the first time, you may be confused about the correct size of rings that you should buy. Keep in mind that in chain maille you are going to put rings into other rings. So it is the ID or inner diameter of the rings that is most important. The number of rings that you can put in another ring depends on how much space is there within the ring.

4. Open and close the jump rings correctly

It is important to open and close the jump rings correctly. When opening, do not pull the ends in opposite directions to try to open the ring. If you do this you may spoil the shape of the ring. You should twist the ends when you want to open or close the rings. If you do not close the rings properly all your hard work may be wasted because the rings may fall apart.

5. Handle the rings carefully

Do not open or close the rings, again and again, multiple times. If you do this too many times they may become brittle or break. Open some jump rings and keep them in separate piles before you start linking them. You can label the piles if you want. This ensures that you will handle them only once or twice and there will be less chance of damaging them in the process.

Another important thing is that you should not tumble the anodized aluminum rings because their color may wear off.

6. Have some extra supplies

You should always have some extra jump rings, more than what is specified in the pattern, while doing a chain maille project. As a beginner, you may not be so adept at handling the rings and some may get bent, broken, or lost. When you go to buy them again the rings of the same color or size may be out of stock and you may not be able to get more of them. As a result, your project may remain incomplete.

Buy the rings from one supplier because there are subtle differences between the rings made by different manufacturers. If you substitute rings with slightly different rings throughout, it can make a lot of difference in the weave.

7. Buy saw-cut rings

When you buy jump rings always ask the supplier whether they are machine-made or saw-cut. Machine-made rings have angles and do not close properly. The saw-cut rings have flush-cut ends. So they close perfectly.

8. Organize and store the rings

When you store the jump rings, put them in separate packets and label them. Write the gauge, inner diameter, type of metal, and the supplier or manufacturer information. This will be very handy for you when you want to buy new supplies or wish to work on your various projects.

BIBLIOGRAPHY

7 Easy chain maille tips for successful chain maille jewelry making. (2016, November 17). Retrieved from

https://www.interweave.com/article/jewelry/free-chain-maille-tips/

Aspect ratio and ring sizing. Retrieved from

http://www.chainmaildude.com/store/index.php?route=information/information&information_id=10

Aussie Maille. (2019, March 20). Chain maille basics - How to weave European 4 in 1 (stretchy). Retrieved from

https://www.youtube.com/watch?v=KTJNoO-riQQ

Badea, C.L. (2012, December 12). European 6 in 1 weave tutorial. Retrieved from

http://www.craftycristian.com/european-6-in-1-weave/

Badea, C.L. (2012, December 23). Half Persian 3 in 1 tutorial. Retrieved from

http://www.craftycristian.com/half-persian-3-in-1/

Badea, C.L. (2013, January 4). Half Persian 4 in 1 chainmaille tutorial. Retrieved from

http://www.craftycristian.com/half-persian-4-in-1/

Beadaholique. (2012, May 8). How to make Dragonscale chain maille. Retrieved from

https://www.youtube.com/watch?v=MW-JQ35rs9c

Beaded Jewelry Diva. (2015, August 24). Chain Maille 101 - Intro to chain mail jewelry, part 1. Retrieved from

https://www.youtube.com/watch?v=_thIHKyOEGs&list=PLlrjOezwxajahk4CyWK_ytjjN2HKbIteS&index=4&t=0s

Common chainmaille definitions and abbreviations. Retrieved from

https://www.bluebuddhaboutique.com/b3/faq/chainmaille/terms-and-jargon

European 4 in 1 chain mail. Retrieved from

https://www.artbeads.com/design-studio/european-four-in-one-chain-mail/

Frequently asked questions. Retrieved from

https://www.themetalmark.com/help#t12n102

Gutsy Girl Design. (2017, July 1). The quick and dirty on chainmaille aspect ratio. Retrieved from

https://www.youtube.com/watch?v=2W8RwzMsq5k

Jennifer. (2012, July 27). Getting started with chain maille: 5 Things you need to know. Retrieved from https://www.interweave.com/article/beading/getting-started-with-chain-maille-5-things-you-need-to-know/

Kathy Priday. (2016, April 21). Spiral 4 in 1. Retrieved from

https://www.youtube.com/watch?v=3ag_wzzhB7w

kurnous34. (2006, October 9). How to make chainmaille spiral pattern. Retrieved from

https://www.youtube.com/watch?v=j6rnuP2Y2m0

Measurements, gauges & jewelry terms. Retrieved from

http://www.rings-things.com/Learn/Wire-Chart/

Miron, A. (2016, April 13). Half Persian 4 in 1 chainmail tutorial. Retrieved from

https://www.youtube.com/watch?v=tjb9hG2s380

Nez Designs. (2017, September 30). Easy method half Persian 4 in 1 chainmaille weave tutorial. Retrieved from

https://www.youtube.com/watch?v=odkHvlmq6qY

NiaSkywalk. (2009, July 1). Chain Maille. Retrieved from

https://www.flickr.com/photos/niaskywalk/3706670153/in/photolist-6DxDU6-58LhCi-4jVAJS-a15ewN-4GC7yL-4d6cdP-5uvmc1-9BkUgb-9aAsH8-9qeXNv-4S6DAx-9aDzz5-bSMPG4-5LFSt2-9aAhTt-4SaQzY-r9XnWz-9GJotZ-9aAsgD-9aDceb-9WtQvo-9azXsn-ahCCMc-fD2Axy-4qqSqL-aWJHq8-9qi16m-4oRs7R-5VC4Tv-6teNWX-e86VyF-9aAg5M-dh65ZH-9aDcFw-9aDoRw-CkyRe-aHzppi-7tt6GV-8B9hVK-2rykG7-4xBWYp-4KGQF9-a2sgAk-8F5koS-5wg8f4-CkyR4-698Z17-nfDSR-5VGpbJ-9m4U3y

Opening and closing loops and jump rings. Retrieved from

http://facetjewelry.com/metal-wire/how-to/2016/04/opening-and-closing-loops-and-jump-rings

Richardson, S. (2011, January 17). How - To: Learn Japanese 12 in 2 chain - maille weave in 6 steps. Retrieved from

https://www.interweave.com/article/jewelry/how-to-learn-japanese-12-in-2-chain-maille-weave-in-6-steps/

Shaw, T. (2017, July 15). Easy Byzantine chainmail tutorial - How to make a bracelet.

Retrieved from

https://www.youtube.com/watch?v=-QwD_T9anio

Simple aspect ratio calculator. Retrieved from

https://www.bluebuddhaboutique.com/b3/ring_sizes/aspect_ratio

The ChainMaille Lady. (2011, March 4). Dragonscale bracelet sterling silver & pink niobium. Retrieved from

https://www.flickr.com/photos/thechainmaillelady/5560087101/in/pool---chainmail_jewelery_and_armor--/

What is chainmaille. Retrieved from

https://www.bluebuddhaboutique.com/b3/faq/chainmaille/what-is-chain-maille

What do your ring names mean. Retrieved from

https://www.bluebuddhaboutique.com/b3/faq/ringsize/B3-ring-names

Williams, Y. (2016, December 20). Doubled Spiral Chain Tutorial. Retrieved from

https://www.youtube.com/watch?v=HGHNq7tCzIw

Williams, Y. (2019, June 22). Euro 4 - 1 size variations. Retrieved from

https://www.youtube.com/watch?v=sCgWU-5MWtY

gauges and ring sizes. Retrieved from

https://theringlord.com/cart/shopcontent.asp?type=WireGauge

KUMIHIMO WIRE WEAVING

How to Make Kumihimo Braids With Affordable Metals and Minimal Tools

INTRODUCTION

Kumihimo refers to a type of Japanese method of braiding by which different kinds of stringing materials are used. Often beads are also used to make unique jewelry and home decor items. The meaning of the word Kumihimo is to gather threads. In this technique, a variety of looms are used to make different kinds of braids. There is a vast scope for creativity and countless designs can be made using simple tools.

You can give a new look to your object by using different numbers and colors of strands. The type of stringing materials used can also give an entirely novel look to the piece. Moreover, the beauty of the object can be enhanced by adding beads, magatamas, and cabochons.

You can even use different kinds of wires to make jewelry using Kumihimo techniques. Although there are people who spend a lot of money and buy gold and silver wires for this purpose, you can make items using inexpensive wires, too. You will be surprised to see that even with a simple copper wire you can make exquisite items.

If you are interested in this craft but you are hesitant to take it up because you think it may involve an excessive expenditure, you can throw caution to the wind. This hobby can be pursued using simple tools and inexpensive materials. This book will help you to learn the basics of Kumihimo wire braiding.

If you are a Kumihimo braider and want to start doing projects with wire, then this book will be very useful for you. You will learn how to make various Kumihimo designs with wire. Let's get started!

CHAPTER 1: TOOLS REQUIRED FOR
MAKING WIRE KUMIHIMO

The basic things required for wire Kumihimo are as follows:

Kumihimo Disks Made of Foam

These disks are not expensive and you can easily write on them if you want to mark anything. They are portable and lightweight.

They are available in square and round shapes. Square disks are used for making flat braids. They are suitable for making flat bracelets. The round disks are usually in 4-inch and 6-inch sizes. They are used to make round braids that have a hollow central core.

Kumihimo Bobbins

When making kumihimo braids, you need to manage a number of strands of wire. Plastic bobbins are useful for this purpose. They are also helpful in holding the beads in the right place while braiding.

These bobbins are inexpensive. They are available in most of the local craft shops. You can also buy a set of these bobbins online from a bead supplier.

EZ-Bob Kumihimo bobbins - They are handy small plastic disks that keep the wires from tangling. You can unfold their cover and wind the wire onto them, and then fold the cover back. In this way you can manage the wires easily. Small ones are a little less than two inches in diameter. Large ones are 2.5 inches in diameter. You can get eight small bobbins for around $3.25, and eight large ones for around $3.75.

Copper Wire

You can buy fine-gauge copper wire for your project. The 24 and 26 gauge wire is finer than the 12 gauge wire. So choose the thickness of the wire depending on the type of object you are planning to make. For example, if you wish to make a piece of jewelry it is better to use a 24 or 26 gauge wire while a 12 gauge wire is more suitable for making home decor items. In the beginning you should use 26 gauge soft copper wire for your Kumihimo project.

Zebra wire - Zebra wire is a 30 gauge fine wire used for Kumihimo braiding. It is a copper wire with a beautiful color coating. It has a glossy finish and is strong and flexible. It is available in spools of 50 yards. Each spool costs around $3.95.

Copper Hobby wire - You can buy copper hobby wire that is very suitable for craftwork.

Beads

You can choose different kinds of beads to add to your handcrafted object. In the beginning, it is enough if you have some tubes of seed beads–size 6.

End Caps or Clasps

You can use decorative caps or crimps with loops to cover the ending part of the Kumihimo braids. A variety of end caps are available, and you can choose any shape, metal, and color. You can also use end caps that have a hook or use a magnetic clasp.

Some end caps and clasps that you can use are as follows:

- 3mm and 6mm clasps for flat and round braids. End caps for round braids. Clamps for flat braids. They may have a gold, silver, or copper plating.
- 1/2" plated end clamp–silver–This clamp is used for flat Kumihimo braids. It is a foldover cap that has tiny teeth inside that grip the braid when you flatten this end cap down on the braid ending with pliers. A packet containing 10 clamps costs around $1.95.
- 6mm barrel end caps - They are plated with precious metal. Larger sizes of these caps are suitable for thicker wire braids. You can buy two of them for around $1.25.

Nylon Jaw Pliers

Nylon jaw pliers are useful for preparing the wire for Kumihimo. You can use them to remove the kinks and bends in the wire before you start the work. They can be used to cut the wire and trim it at the end. Moreover, you can turn the ends of the wires after you finish the braid and secure it with the help of these pliers. They are good for craft work as they do not damage the wires.

Adhesive

You will need some glue to attach the end cap or clasps. E6000 Jewelry and Bead Adhesive is suitable for this purpose.

Weight

To maintain an even tension throughout the braiding process you will be required to put some pressure on the central knot. For this, you can attach some kind of weight to the knot in the center of the plate or disk, or attach a small bag of pennies.

Tip: You can cut the foot of a nylon stocking and place the pennies inside for the bag. Tie the end tightly.

Mandrel Cone

When you are making a bracelet, you need to know if you have reached the desired length of the braid. So, it is essential to have a mandrel cone with you when you are making bracelets.

You can use a mandrel cone made of wood to measure the bracelets that you make. The size of a bracelets is measured in inches. But usually the mandrel cones do not have any markings on them. You can take some painter's tape and paste it on the mandrel cone lengthwise. Then take a measuring tape and wrap it around the mandrel cone. Keep sliding it down and mark the various inches on the painter's tape.

In this way, you can know the correct measurements of the braid when you wrap it around the mandrel cone.

Essential Tools for Making a Hollow Kumihimo Braid

Round Kumihimo disk - It is needed for making a round braid.

Soft copper wire 20 gauge - This type of wire is easier to move around on the disk.

Wooden dowel 6mm in diameter - It acts as the core of the braid and helps to create an even hollow braid. It maintains an empty space inside the braid where you can place beads of the same diameter later if you want.

A small metallic hook - You have to put the hook at the end of the dowel to use it for braiding. You can screw it in and take it out later.

First you have to attach the wires to the hook and secure them. For example, you can take four pieces of 31-inch copper wire. Fold the wires into half and turn their center around the hook once so that they remain there. Then put the hook into the central hole of the disk and hold it between your fingers underneath the disk. After that you can attach the weight to it.

Once you have completed the braid you can screw out the hook and take out the dowel gently from the braid. In this way you can create a hollow braid with wire using these essential tools.

CHAPTER 2: 10 KUMIHIMO HACKS TO MAKE IT EASY TO LEARN

Using wire for braiding is quite different from doing Kumihimo with other materials. Wire is firmer than other materials. So, you need some practice to perfect this craft. With practice you can become familiar with all the nuances of the wire, and you will be able to accomplish gorgeous results. You can create striking pendants, statement earrings, and stunning bracelets just by moving wires repetitively on a Kumihimo disk or plate.

A positive point of using wire for this craft is that wire maintains its shape. So you can take a break from your work at any time without worrying that it may get ruined if you leave it halfway.

Here are some useful techniques that can help you in improving your skill in doing Kumihimo wirework.

Prepare the Wire

If you prepare the copper wire properly, it will be much easier to move it around on a Kumihimo disk. To make it ready for braiding you have to straighten, secure, and sometimes twist it.

Straightening the Wire

Before cutting the wire for any project you have to straighten it and remove all the bends and kinks. If there are crinkles, the wire can become weak. It can also spoil the overall appearance of the final braid.

You can straighten the wire using different methods. It is recommended that you straighten the wire when it is attached to a spool. The reason for this is that it is much easier to hold a spool and straighten the wire instead of holding short pieces of wire in the hand and straightening them.

Use your fingers - You can smooth the curves by moving your fingers over the wire a few times, or pinch it. This also helps to warm it up and makes it more convenient to manipulate and straighten it.

Use nylon pliers - With this method you can use nylon pliers to straighten out the curves. If you use these pliers you can have a much better grip and also straighten tough wires.

Secure the Wire

You should use electrical tape and secure the wires. This will prevent them from crisscrossing while braiding.

After cutting the wires for any project, lay them in a line. See to it that their ends are lined up evenly. Cut a one-and-one-half inch to two-inch piece of electrical tape. Put it near the ends of all the wires. There should be a small length of the wires that should stick out under the tape, maybe around one-fourth inch. Wrap the electrical tape tightly around the wires. Make sure that the lengths lie flat near one another.

Twisted Wire

You can use twisted wire for your Kumihimo projects because it gives a unique look to the object. You can easily twist the wire yourself or buy some twisted wire. Besides this, there are a number of tools available for twisting the wires. While working with twisted wires you must remember that when the wires are twisted their length will decrease around 10 percent.

If you want to make your own twisted wire take a long wire and fold it in half. If you do this less wire will be wasted and there will be a loop at one end. This loop can be attached to something in a secure manner; for example, it can be attached to the door handle. After that, its open ends can be joined to a drill or some tool that twists wire. You can twist the particular wire according to your liking, but do not twist it excessively as it may break. After the work is done slide off from the doorknob. Cut off the loop as well as the bent portion of the wire before using it for braiding.

Use Inexpensive Wire for Practice

To gain a proper knowledge of the Kumihimo techniques in an easy and economical manner it is best to use inexpensive wire such as a copper wire. You can get used to the various braiding techniques and discover the method of making basic braids by using such wires that won't impinge upon your pocket. Moreover, the items made with these wires are quite impressive and have their own charm.

Hold the Kumihimo Disk or Plate Firmly

Hold the disk firmly. Your fingers should be very near the disk's back while braiding. One hand should have a firm grip on the disk while the other hand should move the wires. As the braid becomes bigger, see to it that your fingers remain very near the disk's back side. In case you feel that the braid is misshapen under the disk, straighten it and then proceed.

Maintain the Correct Level of Tension

It is important to achieve and maintain the correct level of tension while using wire for making braids. It is better to make it tightly. If there is less tension the braid might become loose and unmanageable. You will not be able to get the results that you desire. You must aim to have the different wires lying closely against each other while braiding. This will help to create a firm structure that can be shaped. You must practice and learn to maintain the correct tension while braiding with wire.

Tame the Wire

Compared to fiber, wire responds quite differently. Fiber is soft. It can be moved easily. Therefore, it is much easier to create a tight and even braid. Wire is harder and it is not so easy to take it around a disk and make a pattern. It is difficult to make a fully closed braid with it. But there are some specific ways you can tame the wire and make it move in the way you want it to, and make a fairly even and tight braid structure. Show the wire that you are the boss.

Here are some ways you can achieve this:

- When you move the wire from the north or south of the Kumihimo disk toward the east or west sides, pull it tightly and press it down near the ending part of a braid so that it sits near the rest of the wires.
- When you move the wire from the southern to the northern part of the disk, use your thumb and press that wire on the rest of the wires, over which the wire is crossing, at the ending part of a braid. Do the same thing while taking the wires from the north to the south. But this time, instead of using the thumb, press the wire with the index finger.
- When there is a wire that is on the east or west side and has to be brought back into a braid, you can use the thumb or index finger and press the braid's side as you move the wire toward the north or south. Depending on the structure of the braid, you can use both hands alternatively while making these moves with the wire.
- Every time before moving a wire from one slit to another, run it through your fingers. This will enable you to straighten out the kinks and bends that may appear in a wire while moving it around on the disk. It will also prevent the wire from getting damaged or breaking.

Sometimes the wires lying next to one another may start overlapping on the Kumihimo disk. This is quite normal. It will not have any impact on the finished braid if the wires have been put in the correct slits according to the pattern.

Take Notes

Whenever you make a Kumihimo project you must make it a point to note down all the things you used, and if you ran short of anything, what mistakes you made and any other relevant things that may be useful for reference when you do your future projects. This will help you to learn from direct experience and prevent you from making the same mistakes every time.

These are the things you can do while taking notes:

- You can give a name to your braid.
- Trace the outline of the bobbin you used.
- Draw a disk and mark the way in which the wires are positioned.
- Note the types and colors of wire you used.
- Note how long the wires were that you cut.
- If you used beads, note which wires you strung the beads.
- Note how many grams or bags of beads you used.
- Mention the size and type of end caps you used.
- Write down anything that is worth remembering. Mention if the wire was too short or too long.

Check the Work Frequently

It can be very disappointing if after completing the braid you find that you have made a mistake somewhere and your item looks skewed. So it is better to check the work as you progress and make corrections there rather than completing the work in haste and redoing it all over again.

This is especially important when you are using beads. If you miss just one bead it can ruin your entire project. Therefore, be attentive and check if your work looks all right. If the beads do not align properly or something looks misshapen, be smart enough to check and correct the mistake on the spot. This will actually save time and help you to achieve your goal of making an impressive and flawless object.

Start from the Middle

If you want to make a necklace with one focal bead that has a hole that's very small for a finished braid to pass, you can start the project from the middle. You can start braiding from the center and make half of the necklace, and again make the braid from the center to the other end.

CHAPTER 3: KUMIHIMO PLATE AND DISK

After the Kumihimo plate and disk made of polyethylene foam were invented by a person named Makiko Tada Kumihimo, the craft of Kumihimo beading has become more accessible and more popular. These plates and disks are available in various sizes with different thicknesses and diameters.

The Kumihimo Plate

The braids made on the Kumihimo plate resemble the braids made on the takadai. The square Kumihimo plate is perfect for making square and flat braids.

The Kumihimo Disk

The braids made using the Kumihimo disk resemble the braids made on the marudai. The disk can be used to make both round and square braids. It can also be used to make flat braids that are narrow.

Hamanaka Disk

The original Hamanaka Disk, which has a diameter of six inches, has a thickness of 10mm (⅜ inch). It has a dense foam that provides the right tension for holding the wires.

BeadSmith Mini

BeadSmith Mini has a similar thickness like Hamanaka but has a diameter of 4.25 inches. This can be used by kids and adults alike. You can use it to make the same braids like the 6-inch diameter disk. It is easier to carry it around wherever you go.

Thick Mini (BeadSmith)

Thick Mini (BeadSmith) has a diameter of 4.25 inches. It has a double thickness of 20mm (13/16 inch). It is suitable for finer cords as it provides consistent tension.

CHAPTER 4: BASIC ROUND BRAID

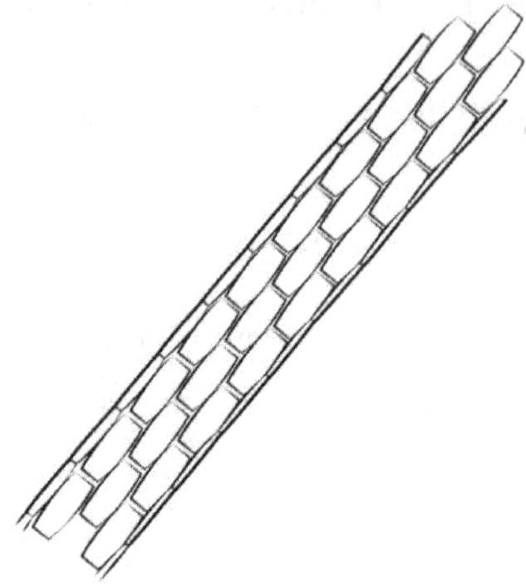

8

Round Braid with 8 Warps

Things You Will Need

- Round Kumihimo disk
- 26 gauge soft copper wire
- 6 mm barrel end caps
- E6000 Jewelry and Bead Adhesive
- Nylon jaw pliers
- Some kind of weight or a small bag full of pennies.
- Nymo string

Instructions

In Kumihimo, the word warp refers to the thread or wire put in a single "slit." In this design, eight warps are used. A general rule to find how much wire will be needed is to take three times the length of the final object you are planning to make. But if you use large beads you may have to increase the length a bit.

Step 1

Set up the Kumihimo disk

Gather the eight strands of wire and tie one knot or turn the ends together and secure them together at one end.

Step 2

---

[8] Getting started with Kumihimo. Retrieved from

https://www.artbeads.com/design-studio/kumihimo-getting-started/

Put the end with the knot in the hole in the center of the disk.

Step 3

Divide the strands into four with two-two in each group. Lay them on the black dots on the disk. When you are positioning the strands see to it that number 32 is on top.

Step 4

Start with 32. Put one-one strand of wire on both sides of the black dot. Pull the wire gently into each slit. Do not pull very hard otherwise the disk may get damaged.

Step 5

Move across the round disk and put the strands of wire into the slits on both sides of number 16. Sufficient tension should be on the wires so that the knot remains in the central hole of the disk.

Step 6

Move toward the right side of your Kumihimo disk and put one strand of wire in the slit next to the dot beside number 8 and another strand on the other side of 8.

Step 7

Then move toward the left and put one-one strand each in the slits beside the black dot near number 24. After all the eight strands of wire have been positioned, the knot should still be centered in the hole of the disk.

Finally, the disk should look like this:

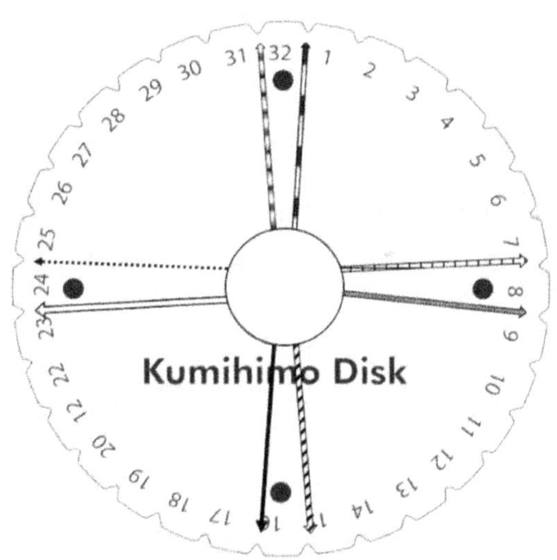

Step 8

Start the braid.

Note: Whenever the number of a slit is mentioned, please use the slit that is on the left side of the number.

It is advisable to put some weight on the central knot, especially when you start braiding so that the braid is tight and uniform. You can hold the knot with your hand and gently pull it down while you make the braid, but it will be easier if you tie a tiny bag filled with some pennies to the central knot. In this way, both your hands will be free to do the braiding.

Step 9

Move the wire in slit number 17 up and take it across the Kumihimo disk to number 31 slit.

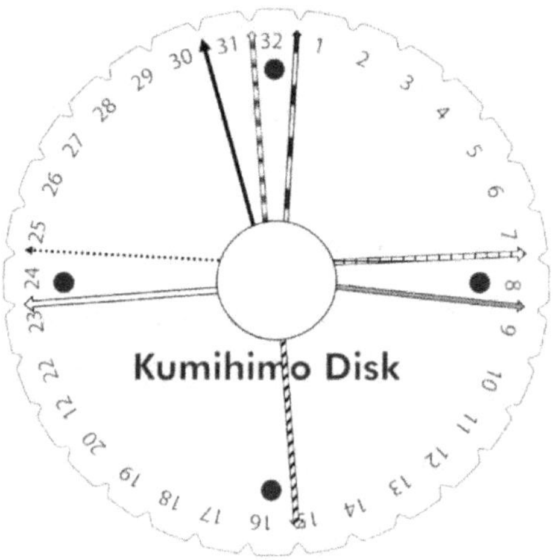

Step 10

Then move the wire in slit 1 across the Kumihimo disk to number 15 slit. You should remember to maintain the same tension all through the process so that the braid is even and there are no bumps.

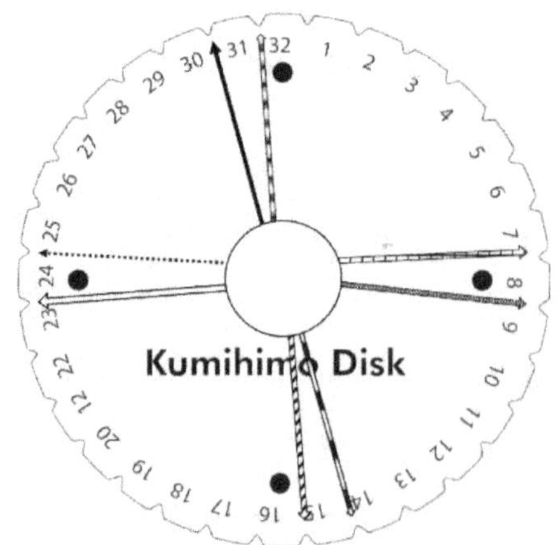

Step 11

After that, turn the disk clockwise one-fourth turn. Now the black dot near number 24 must be on top.

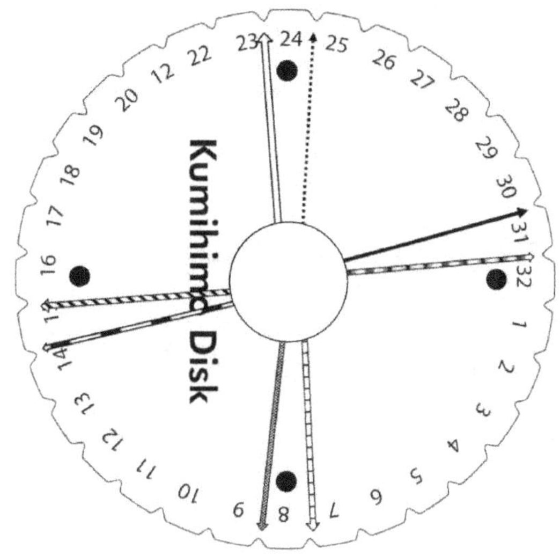

Step 12

Move the wire in 9 to number 23 slit. Take the wire in slit 25 across toward slit 7.

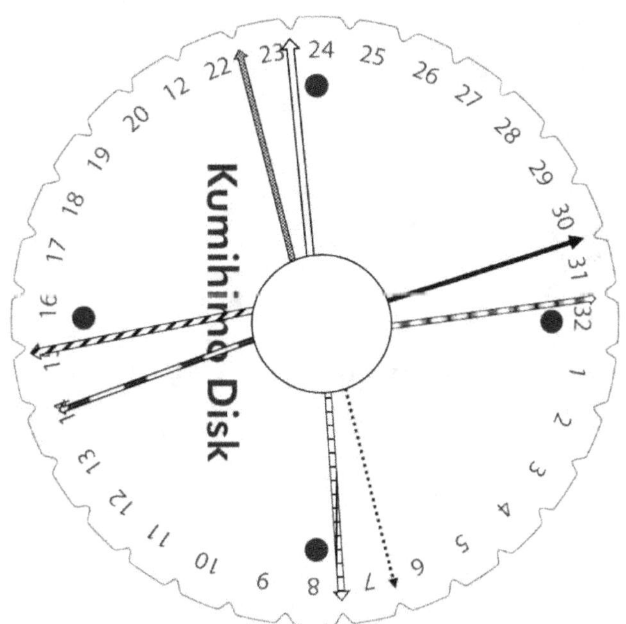

Step 13

Again, turn the Kumihimo disk clockwise one-fourth turn.

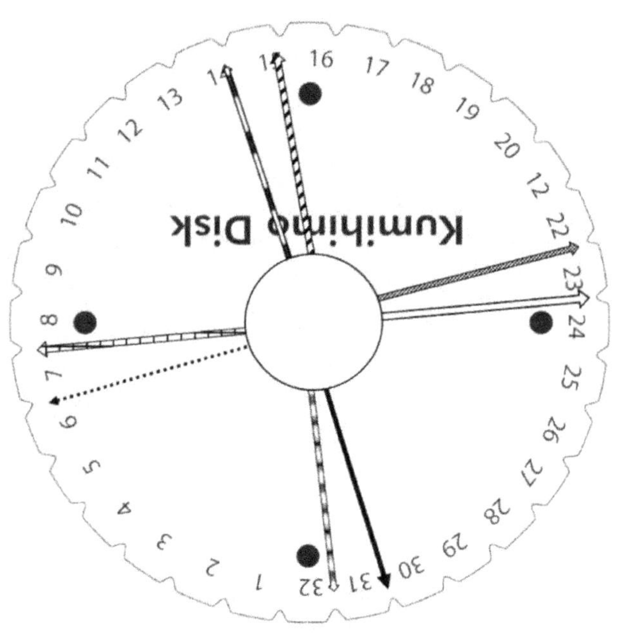

Step 14

Go up and then left. Go down and then right.

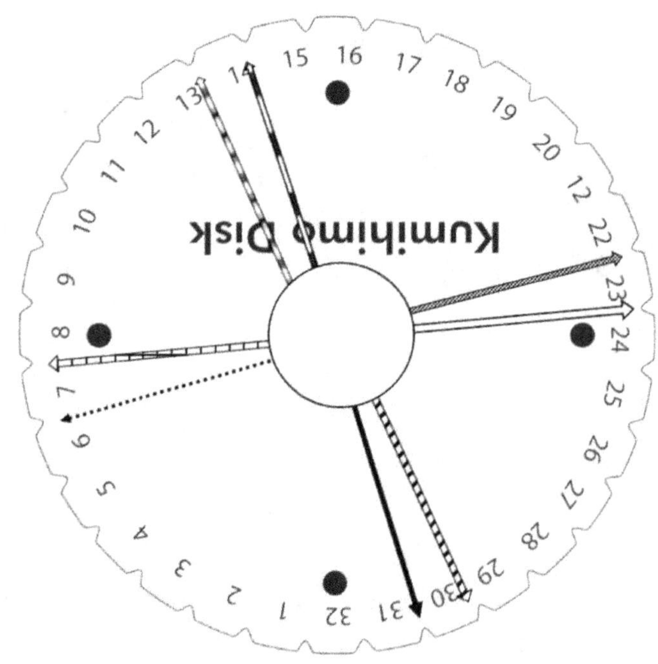

And again, turn the Kumihimo disk clockwise one-fourth turn.

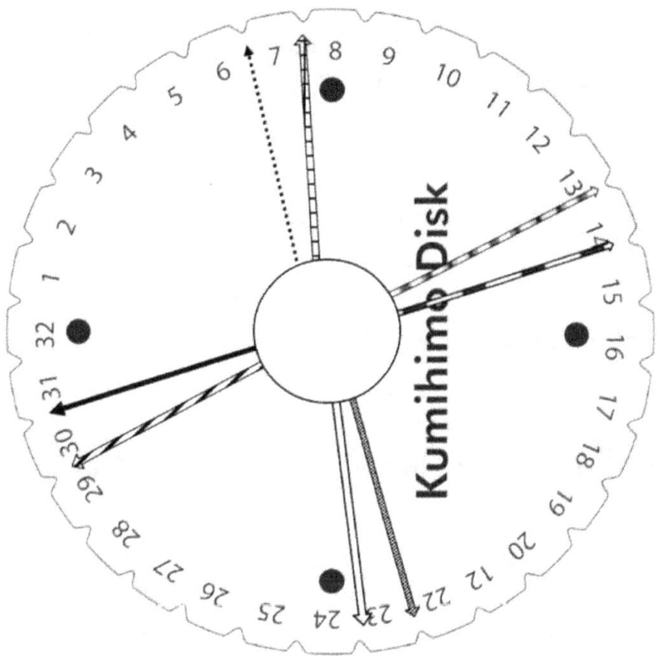

Go up and then left. Go down and then right.

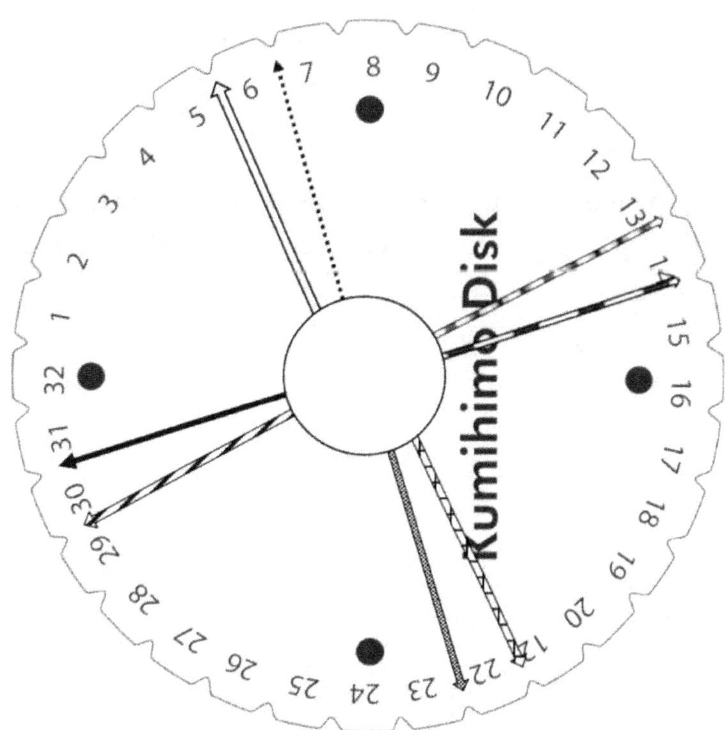

After you have done this around the Kumihimo disk a few times, the numbers will not matter much.

Step 15

You should continue to do the steps until the piece is as big as you want it to be. The length of the object will depend on the design as well as the way in which the finishing of the ends will be done.

Step 16

Take out the braid that you have made from the Kumihimo disk. Tie one knot at the end of the wires.

Step 17

Use a Nymo string, tie one knot at the ending part of the braid.

Step 18

Hold the Nymo string's end and wrap it tightly around the wire braid. Wrap the string's other end in an opposite direction.

Step 19

Again, tie a knot and remove the extra Nymo string using one thread burner.

Step 20

Remove the knot that you had tied with the wire at the end of the braid.

Step 21

Then cut the ending part so that you can attach the end piece. Here you can use one barrel end-cap that has a loop.

Step 22

You can slide this barrel end cap on the ending part of the wire braid so that the Nymo string is covered and then press the end cap with the help of pliers. Put the other end cap on the other end.

CHAPTER 5: KONGO GUMI

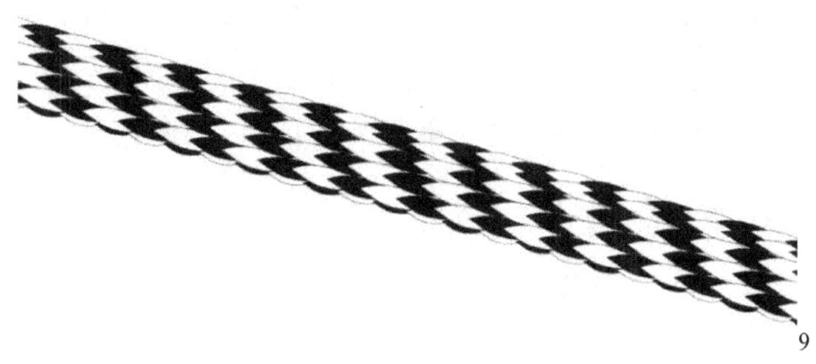

[9]

Kongo Gumi is also known as spiral braid.

Things You Will Need

- Round Kumihimo disk
- 26 gauge soft copper wire
- 6 mm barrel end caps
- E6000 Jewelry and Bead Adhesive
- Nylon jaw pliers
- Some kind of weight or a small bag full of pennies.

Instructions

It is the same as the basic round braid, but with 2 different colors of wire.

Take 2 lengths of wire, 1 yard each. Make sure that they are of different colors. Fold them into half and cut them at the center to make four lengths of wire.

Step 1

Fold the wires into half and tie them together at the center using another wire. Attach a weight to this knot that you have tied with the extra wire. This will help to maintain the right tension while braiding. Then take some scrap wire and tie it around all the wires at this end so that it will be easy to finish the ends neatly.

Step 2

Put the knotted end into the central hole of the kumihimo disk. Hold it with your index finger and thumb under the disk.

---

[9] Redmond, N. (n.d.). Braiding disk instructions. Kumihimo tutorials for making round braids on a braiding disk. Retrieved from

https://www.weircrafts.com/kumihimo/kumihimo-instructions/kumihimo-disk-instructions/spiral-braid.html

Step 3

Place the wires on the disk in such a way that two wires of color #1 are on either side of the black dot in the north direction, and two wires are on either side of the black dot in the south direction. That means the wires should be in slit 32 and slit 1 in the north and in slit 16 and slit 17 in the south.

Similarly, place two wires of color #2 on either side of the black dot in the east and two wires on either side of the black dot in the west. That means the wires should be in slit 8 and slit 9 in the east and in slit 24 and slit 25 in the west.

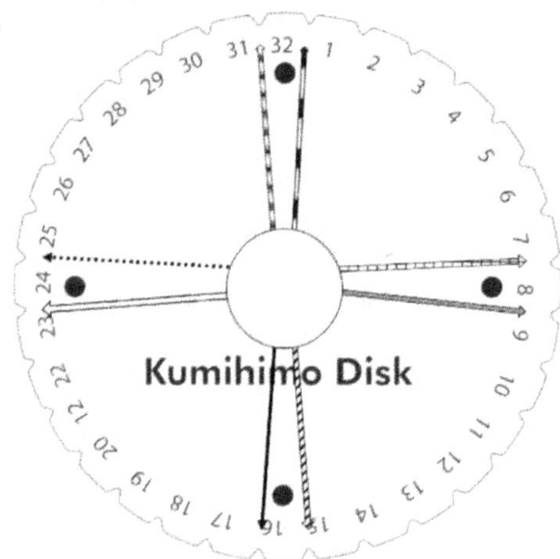

If you are working with longer lengths you can wrap the other ends of the wires in bobbins so that they do not get entangled at the bottom while braiding.

Step 4

Start braiding. The process for spiral braiding - left up, right down, turn.

Take the wire that is in slit 17 and move it to slit 31.

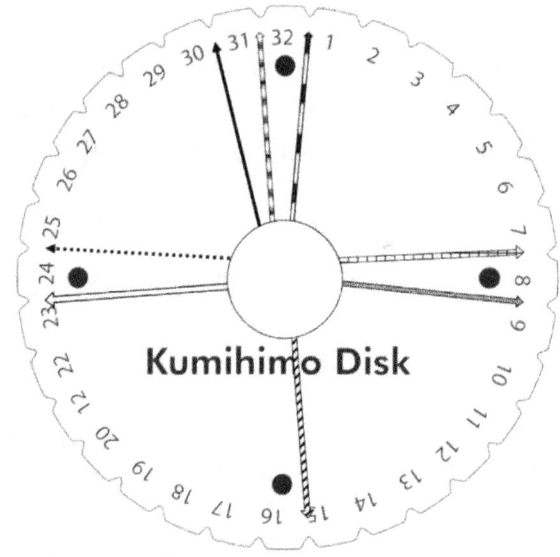

Then move the wire from slit 1 to slit 15.

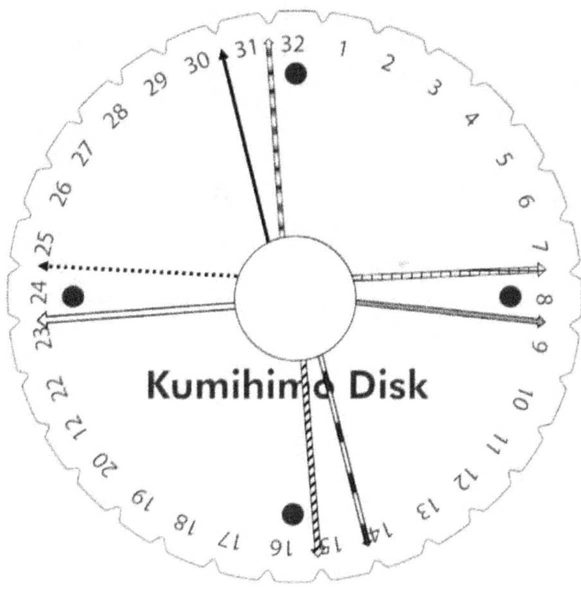

Step 5

Turn the disk so that the east and west wires take the north and south position. You can turn the disk to the right or left as long as you are consistent.

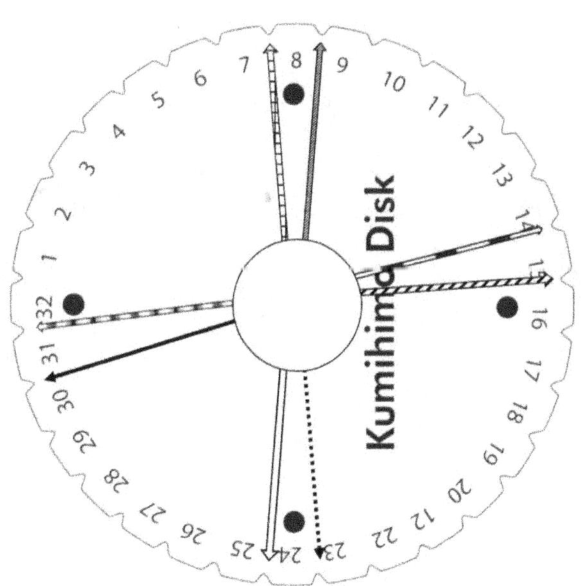

Move the wire from slit 25 to slit 7.

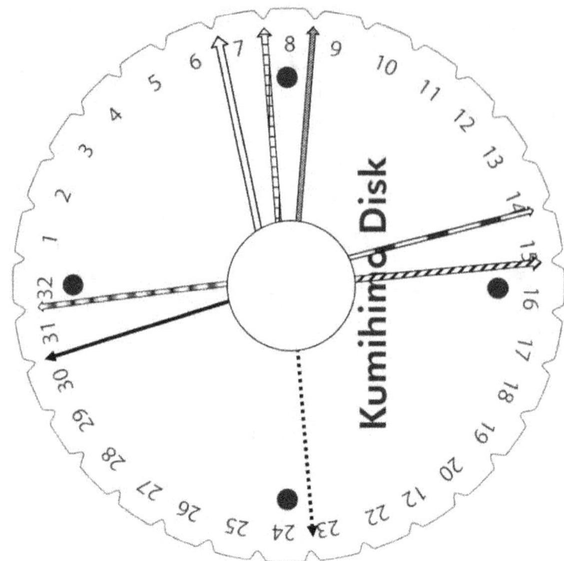

Then move the wire from slit 9 to slit 23.

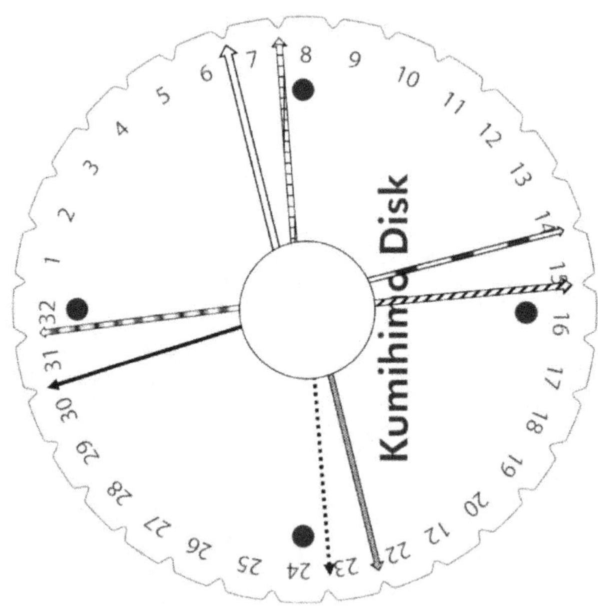

Step 6

Turn the disk so that the north and south directions of the disk come back to their original position. Repeat steps 4 and 5 until you reached the desired length of the braid.

Then remove the braid from the disk and tie all wires together at the end with scrap wire. Cut the extra parts of the wires. After that you can attach end caps at both the ends.

Reversed Kongo Gumi or Spiral Braid

You can rotate the disk in the clockwise direction and change the way in which the wires are moved to make a reversed Kongo Gumi. The spiral's direction in the previous braid resembles the capital letter "Z." Therefore, it is also referred to as the "Z" spiral. While the one that is going to be made here has a spiral that goes in the opposite direction, it is also known as the "S" spiral.

Step 1

Position the wires in the same way as you did for the previous Kongo Gumi.

Step 2

Move the wire on the left-hand side of the north positioning dot. Place it on the left side of the wires in the south.

Move the wire on the right side of the black positioning dot in the south. Place it on the right-hand side of the wire in the north.

Step 3

Rotate the disc in the clockwise direction so that the pair of wires in the north-west and the south-east take the north and south position.

Exchange the places of the wires as you did in step 2.

Keep rotating the disc clockwise again and again. Exchange the places of the wires according to step 2. Complete the braid and attach a cap or clasp at the end.

Zigzag Design

You can change the direction you are braiding and create one zigzag design.

To change direction from "S" spiral and go to the "Z" spiral make the moves mentioned here.

Step 1

Move each right-hand wire over its neighbor before you begin making "Z" spiral.

Step 2

Braid in "Z" pattern. It is same as the first Kongo Gumi braid.

Step 3

Go back and make a zigzag across the wires. This time move the left wires over their right neighbors.

Step 4

Braid in "S" pattern. It is same as the reversed Kongo Gumi braid.

Repeat steps one to four and complete the braid.

CHAPTER 6: EDO YATSU GUMI

Edo Yatsu Gumi is also known as the Checker Braid. [10]

Things You Will Need

- Round Kumihimo disk
- 26 gauge soft copper wire
- Zebra wire
- 6 mm barrel end caps
- E6000 Jewelry and Bead Adhesive
- Nylon jaw pliers
- Some kind of weight or a small bag full of pennies.

Instructions

Round 1

Step 1

Place and secure the wire on the Kumihimo disk in such a way that there are two pairs of plain copper wire on either side of the left and right black positioning dots.

Put plain copper wire on the left side of the black positioning dot onto the topmost part of the disk. Place plain copper wire on the right side of the black positioning dot onto the lowermost part of the disk.

Put the zebra wire in the slit on the right-hand side of the topmost dot and in the slit on the left-hand side of the lowermost dot.

---

[10] Redmond, N. (n.d.). Braiding disk instructions. Kumihimo tutorials for making round braids on a braiding disk. Retrieved from

https://www.weircrafts.com/kumihimo/kumihimo-instructions/kumihimo-disk-instructions/checker-braid.html

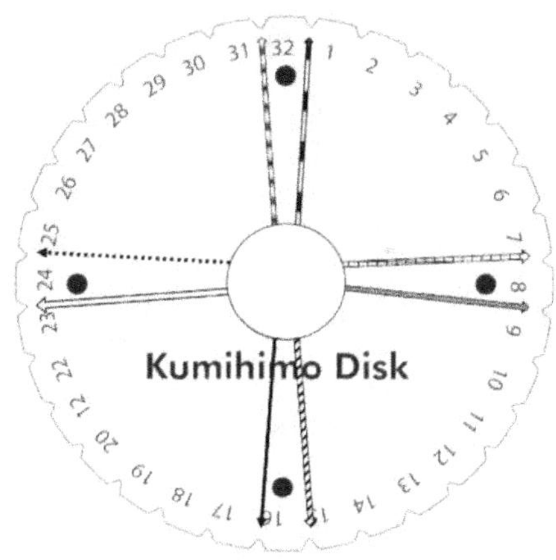

Step 2

Move the plain copper wire from the topmost dot. Make it skip over the zebra wire and place it near the two wires on the right side.

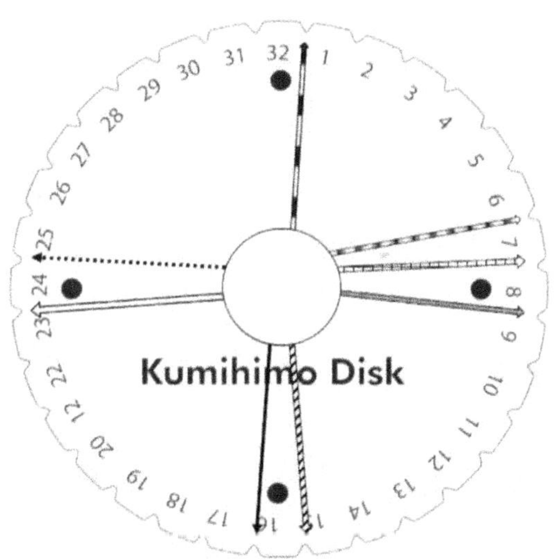

Step 3

Move the lower copper wire on left. Make it skip over its neighboring wire. Move it and place it to the left of the zebra wire at the top.

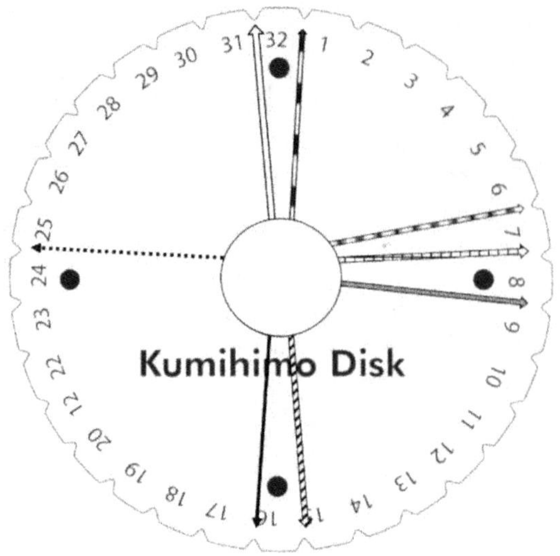
Kumihimo Disk

Step 4

Move the wire on the right of the lowermost dot. Make it skip over its neighboring zebra wire and place it below the left positioning dot.

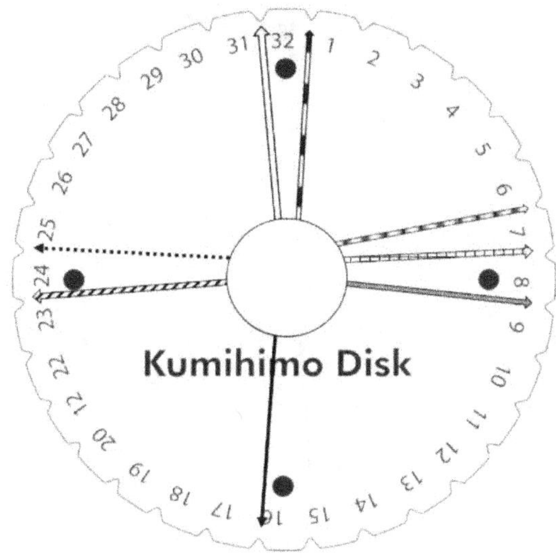

Step 5

Move the wire that is placed in the center of three wires on the right side. Make it skip over the next wire and place it on the right side of the lowermost positioning dot near the single zebra wire.

You will notice that in these moves the wire that is being moved skips over one wire and moves in the clockwise direction.

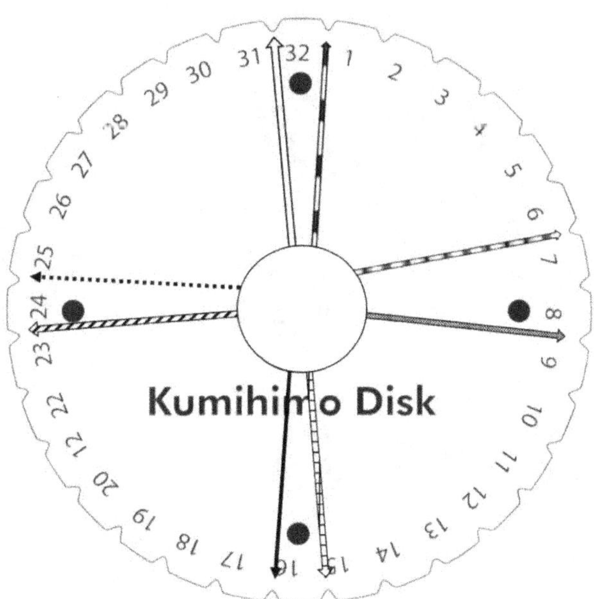

Step 6

Move the upper right-hand side wire down and place it in the slit next to its neighbor.

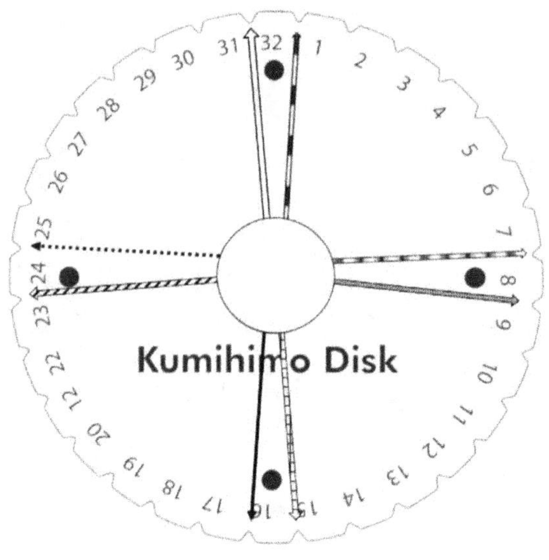

Round 2

Step 1

Move the lower right-hand side wire. Make it skip over the wire adjacent to it and place it on the right side of the zebra wire on the top.

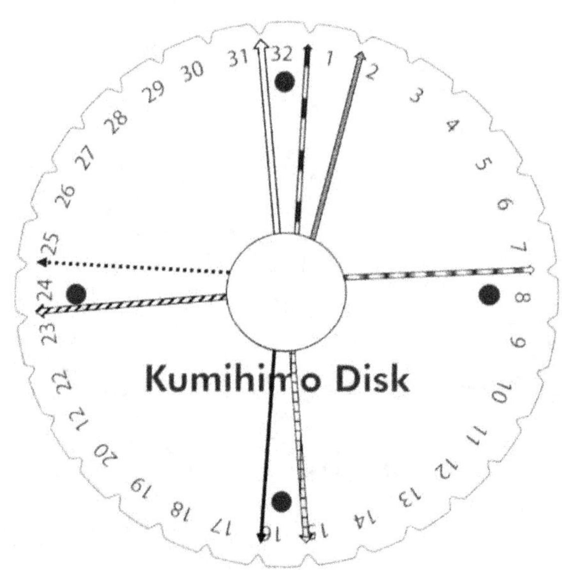

Step 2

Move the lower zebra wire. Make it skip over the next wire and place it on the left side of the right positioning dot.

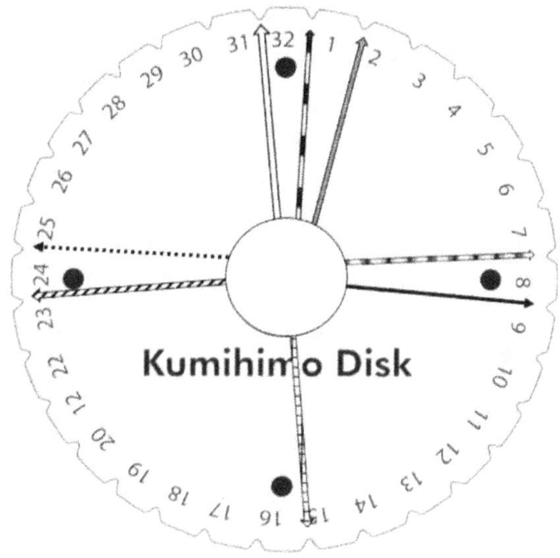

Step 3

Move the upper left-hand side wire. Make it skip over the neighboring wire and place it on the left side of the lower single wire.

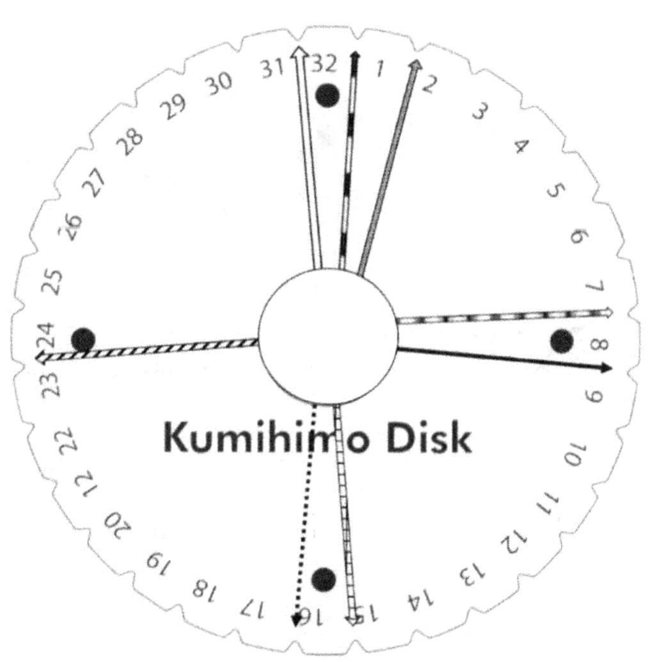

Step 4

Move the top zebra wire. Make it skip over the neighboring wire and place it above the left positioning dot.

You will notice that in the above moves the wires skipped over the adjacent wires in the anti-clockwise direction.

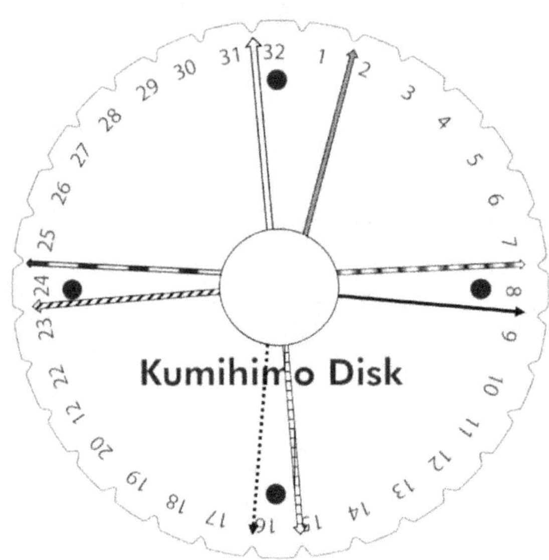

Step 5

Move the top right-hand side wire by one slit. Place it in the slit next to the top positioning dot.

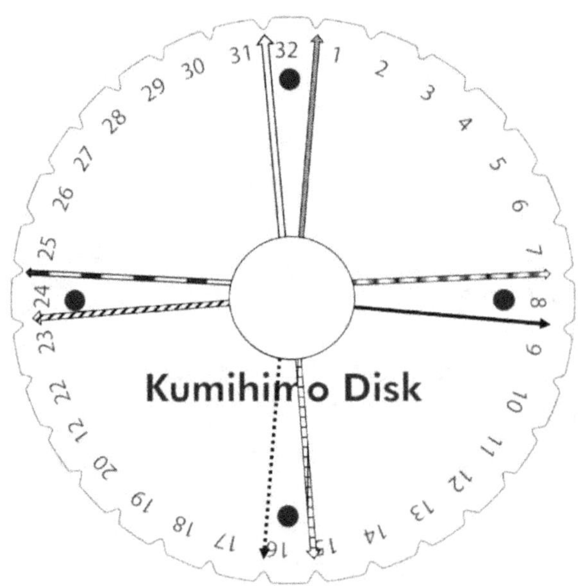

Repeat the two rounds, again and again, to continue making the braid.

CHAPTER 7: HIRA YATSU GUMI

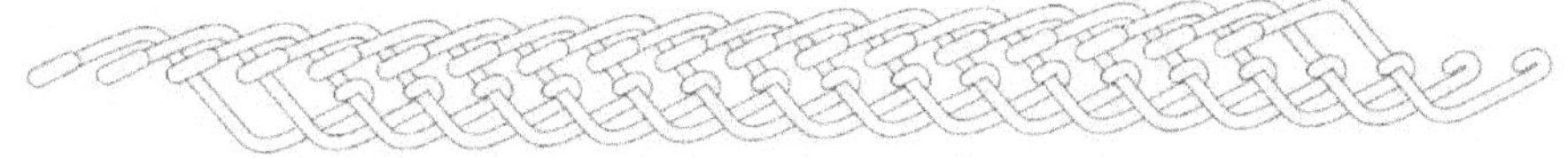

11

Hira Yatsu Gumi - Flat Kumihimo

Flat braids are easy to make and can be used in several ways. You can make a belt or a headband with it. Otherwise, you can utilize it as the basis for your bracelets and necklaces. You can follow the steps given here and create a beautiful flat braid.

Things You Will Need

- Square Kumihimo disk
- 26 gauge soft copper wire
- 6 mm clasps
- E6000 Jewelry and Bead Adhesive
- Nylon jaw pliers
- Some kind of weight or a small bag full of pennies.

Instructions

The square disk has capital letters on the left side and small letters on the right side. Numbers are given at the top and at the bottom. These numbers and letters are important for following the instructions given for any pattern.

You should cut 10 pieces of wire. They should be 20-inches long. Gather all the wires and tape their ends together or tie a knot at the end.

Step 1

This knot should be placed in the disk's central hole.

Step 2

Arrange the wires on the disk in such a way that there are 6 wires in the north and 4 wires in the south. That means that the wires should be in slits 3, 4, 5, 6, 7, 8 at the top. They should be in slits 14, 15, 16, 17 at the bottom.

---

[11] How to do flat Kumihimo. Retrieved from

https://www.artbeads.com/design-studio/flat-kumihimo-braid-handy-tip/

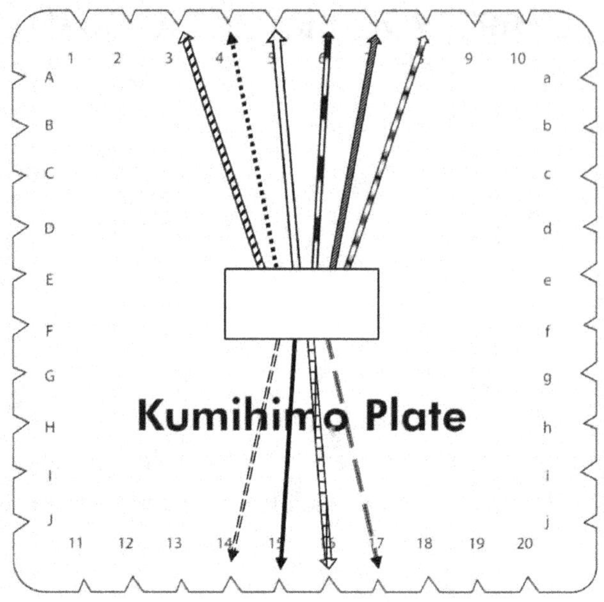

Step 3

To maintain an even tension during braiding, some kind of weight should be attached to the central knot. You can use a small bag of pennies for this purpose.

Step 4

Now you can start the braiding process. Move the wire from slit 5 to slit e. Move wire from slit 6 to slit E. Pay attention and see whether it has to be moved to a capital letter or a small letter according to the pattern.

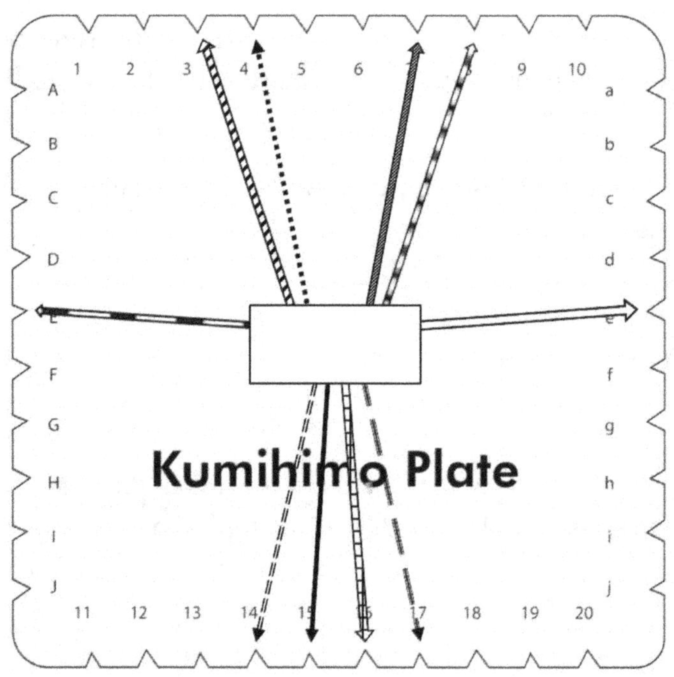

Step 5

Move the wire from slit 15 to slit 5. Move the wire from slit 4 to slit 15.

the pattern.

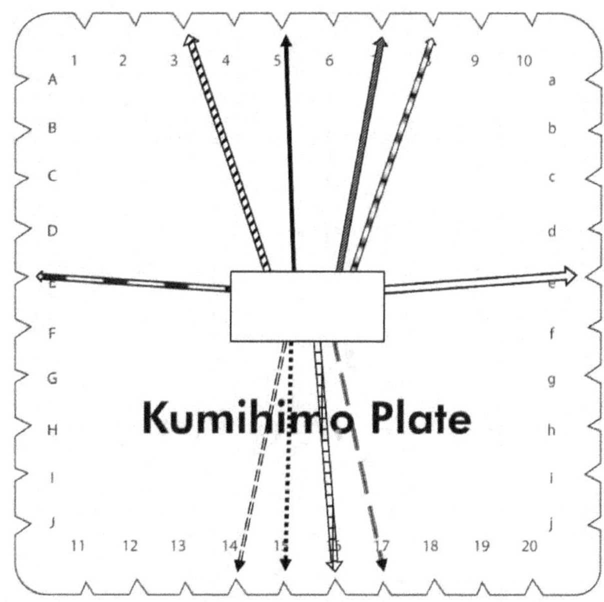

Step 6

Move the wire from slit 14 to slit 4. Move the wire from slit 3 to slit 14.

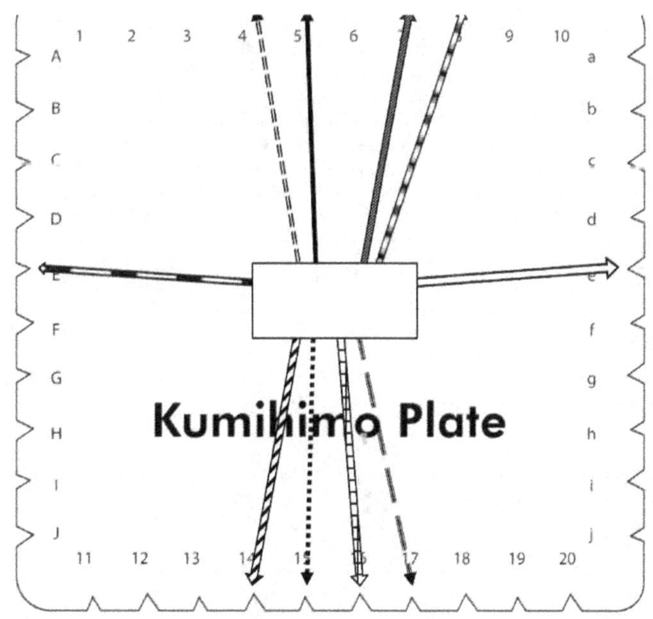

Step 7

Take the wire from slit 16 to slit 6. Move the wire from slit 7 to slit 16.

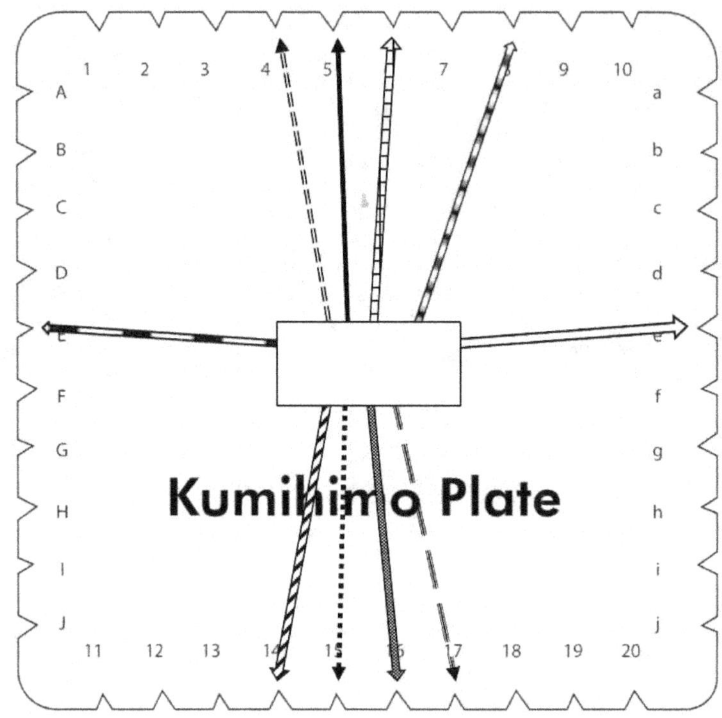

Step 8

Take the wire from slit 17 to slit 7. Move the wire from slit 8 to slit 17.

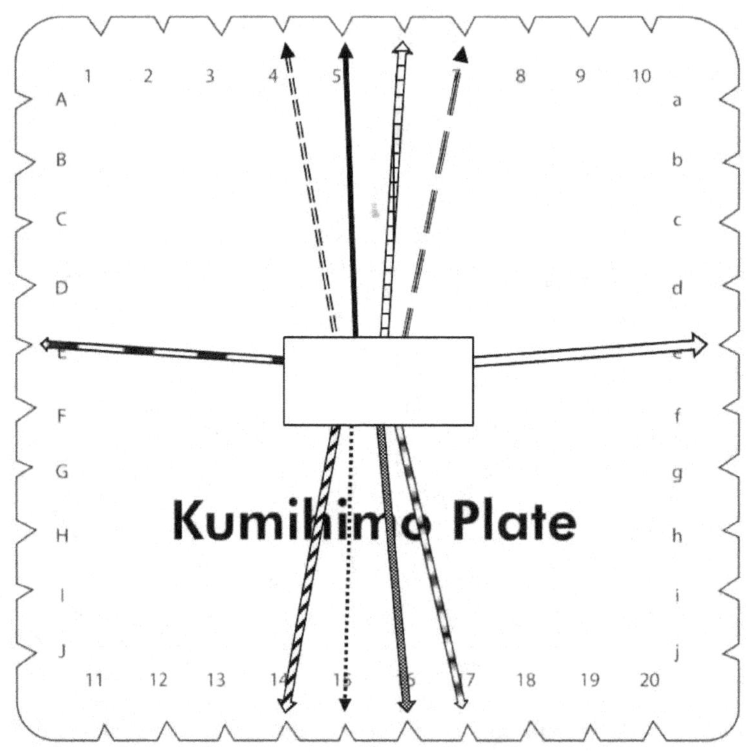

Step 9

Move the wire from slit e to slit 8. Move the wire from slit E to slit 3.

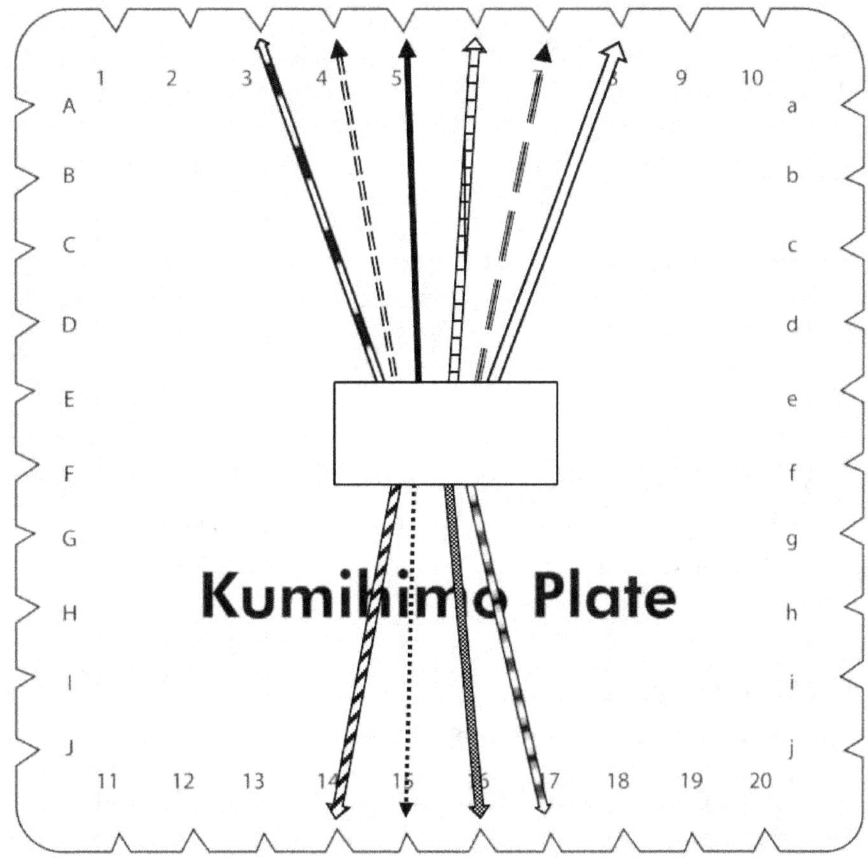

Repeat the steps from step 4 to step 9 and continue braiding until you reach the desired length. Then remove the braid from the disk and gather all the ends of the wires and tie a knot or tape them.

CHAPTER 8: 8 WARP YURUGI GUMI

Things You Will Need

- Round Kumihimo disk
- 26 gauge soft copper wire
- 6 mm clasps
- E6000 Jewelry and Bead Adhesive
- Nylon jaw pliers
- Some kind of weight or a small bag full of pennies.

Instructions

Step 1

Cut 4 pieces of wire. They should be three times the length of the braid that you want to make. Fold them into half and tie them at the center using an extra wire. Place this knot in the central hole of the disk. Then attach some weight to this knot with the extra wire.

Step 2

Hold the knot below the disk with your fingers and arrange the wires on the disk in such a manner that there is one-one wire on either side of the black positioning dots on all the four sides.

That means the wires should be in slits 1 and 32 in the north, slits 16 and 17 in the south, slits 8 and 9 in the east, and slits 24 and 25 in the west.

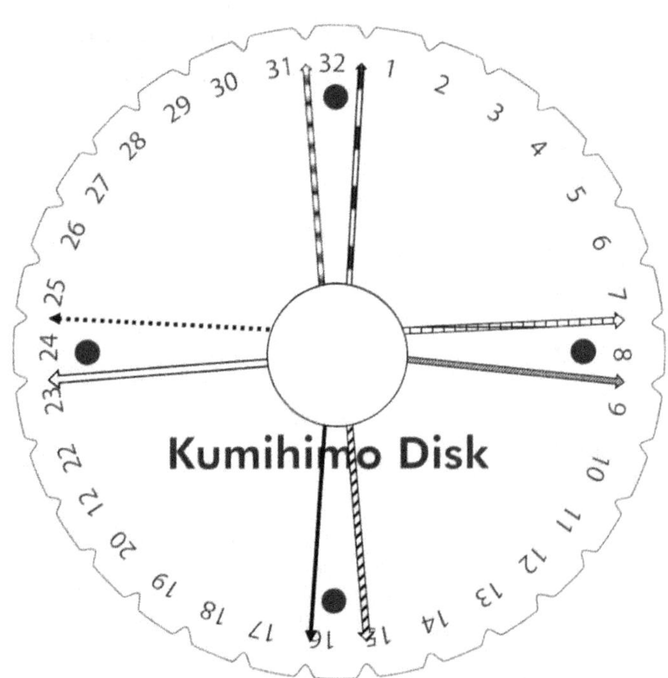

Step 3

Move the wire from slit 1 to slit 23. Move the wire from slit 32 to slit 10. Move the wire from slit 17 to slit 7. Move the wire from slit 16 to slit 26.

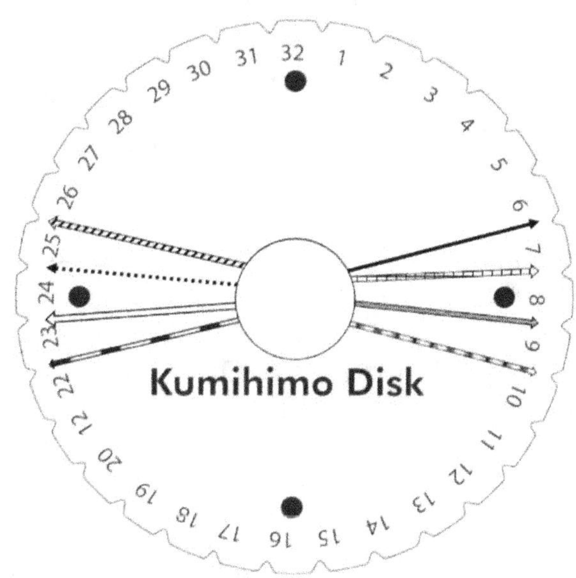

Now all the wires have moved to the east and west. There are no wires in the north and south.

Step 4

Move the wire from slit 25 to slit 17. Move the wire from slit 24 to slit 32. Move the wire from slit 8 to slit 16. Move the wire from slit 9 to slit 1.

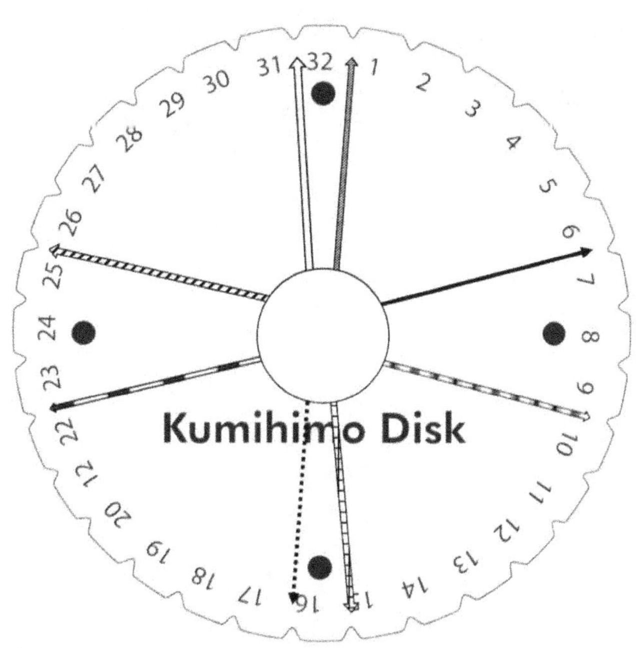

Step 5

Move the wire from slit 26 to slit 25. Move the wire from slit 23 to slit 24. Move the wire from slit 7 to slit 8. Move the wire from slit 10 to slit 9.

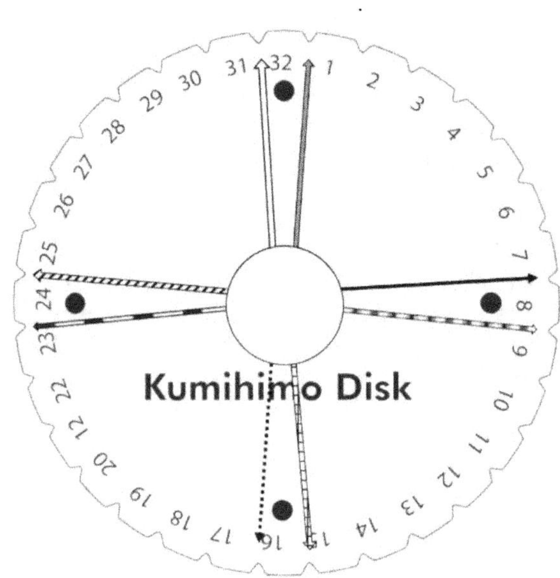

Now there is one-one wire on either side of the black positioning dots on all sides.

Repeat the steps from 3 to 5 and continue braiding until you reach the desired length of the braid.

Then take it out of the disk. Use nylon jaw pliers to cut the extra wires.

Turn the ending part of the wires a bit and secure them. You can put end caps on both the ends to give a neat finish.

Tip: Use nylon jaw pliers to straighten the wire out if your project requires it's

components to fit flush against each other.

BONUS – 12 WARP VERSION:

Instructions

Step 1

Position 12 pieces of wire on the disk in such a way that one pair of wires is on the right side of the black positioning dot in the north and another pair is on the left side of the same dot. That means the wires should be in slits 1, 2, 31, 32.

Similarly, place one pair of wires on the right side of the black positioning dot in the south and another pair on the left side of the dot. So the wires should be in slits 15, 16, 17, 18.

Place one-one wire on either side of the black positioning dot in the east. They should be in slits 8, 9.

In the same way, put one-one wire on either side of the black positioning dot in the west. The wires should be in slits 24, 25.

Step 2

Move the wire from slit 1 to slit 23. Move the wire from slit 32 to slit 10. Move the wire from slit 17 to slit 7. Move the wire from slit 16 to slit 26.

Then move the wire from slit 2 to slit 1. Move the wire from slit 31 to slit 32. Move the wire from slit 15 to slit 16. Move the wire from slit 18 to slit 17.

After that, move the wire from slit 25 to slit 18. Move the wire from slit 24 to slit 31. Move the wire from slit 8 to slit 15. Move the wire from slit 9 to slit 2.

Move the wire from slit 7 to slit 8. Move the wire from slit 26 to slit 25. Move the wire from slit 23 to slit 24.

Repeat the above steps until you reach the desired length of the braid.

Tip: Use nylon jaw pliers to straighten the wire out if your project requires it's

components to fit flush against each other.

CHAPTER 9: USING BEADS IN KUMIHIMO PROJECTS

You can make your object look special and glamorous by adding some beads to it. Depending on your choice of beads, the finished item can have a lovely sparkling hue or be organic and earthy. You can use beads and make jewelry to exhibit your own unique style.

You may choose to scatter just a few beads and let the wire enjoy the spotlight. For this you may put beads in just one or two strands. Or else, you may opt for a complete frontal beadery and put beads in all the strands and make the beads steal the show. You can also mix beads of different sizes to make the texture more attractive.

It does not matter whether you use a naked wire or one that has beads strung on it, the basic Kumihimo stitch, weaving, braiding, and even the wire's length are the same.

How Many Beads are Needed

The number varies and is determined on the basis of approximation. The reason for this is that the sizes of the beads vary slightly even if they belong to the same packet. Moreover, braiding tension varies from one person to another.

On an average basis the number can be as follows:

- You need 6 beads for one inch on every strand if you are using seed beads - size 6, and Delica beads - size 8.
- 7 beads for one inch on every strand if you use seed beads - size 8.
- 9 beads for one inch on every strand while using seed beads - size 11.
- 11 beads for one inch on every strand in case you use Delica beads - size 11.

How to Use Beads

Start by weaving one-fourth inch of the braid with only wire. This will enable you to attach one clasp at the end. When you are finishing the piece, once again make a plain braid.

Step 1

Position the wire on the disk and secure it. After that, string the beads on the wire. Push a few of them to the disk's edge, wrap the rest of the beads inside bobbins.

Step 2

Pick the wire on the left bottom side and slide a bead toward the braid's point.

Step 3

This bead will go under the 1st horizontal wire. Keep it on the outer side of your braid.

Step 4

Let the bead remain under the horizontal wire. Complete your move, insert the wire so there are three wires on top.

Step 5

If the pattern requires you to drop beads in every move, in the next move you should go right and top down. The bead should be moved toward the center of the braid.

Step 6

Slide the bead under, as well as to the outer side of the horizontal cord. Continue braiding and drop beads according to the specifications of the pattern.

Note: Go left and bottom up, then go right and top down, turn clockwise and proceed to the next pair.

Using Colored Beads

To make your project more attractive you can use beads of different colors. You can choose contrasting colors and make a beautiful piece. Otherwise, you may use some beads that have a silver lining with some opaques. Mixing a few black beads and white beads is also a good choice.

Tip: Use a needle to pick up your beads

CHAPTER 10: HOW TO USE CABOCHONS AND MAGATAMAS

Cabochons

In order to add cabochons to your kumihimo project, you should encircle the particular cabochon using the cross-braid structure. You have to use a square plate to make this type of braid.

Beaded Kumihimo Cabochon Earrings

Things You Will Need

- Round Kumihimo disk
- 30 gauge fine copper wire
- Silver grey color 8/0 seed beads
- Black super duos
- Black 15/0 seed beads
- 2 x 3 cm red color oval cabochons
- Black color S-lon size D thread
- Beading needle
- 8 mm Kumihimo ends
- 2 jump rings
- 2 earring findings

Instructions

Cut four pieces of wire 80 cm (31.5 inches) each. Put their ends together and fold them in half. Make a knot at the center. Then attach some scrap wire on the knot. If you want you can attach some weight to the knot.

Put the knot in the central hole of the disk. Position the eight strands of wire on either side of the black dots.

Step 1

Move the wire from slit 32 to slit 18. Move the wire from slit 16 to slit 2. Move the wire from slit 8 to slit 26. Move the wire from slit 24 to slit 10. Move the wire from slit 17 to slit 3. Move the wire from slit 1 to slit 19.

Continue doing this until the braid is 1 to 2 cm long.

Step 2

Start adding the beads. Put super duos with the 8/0 beads in 4 wires. Put only 8/0 beads in four wires.

Top left wire sequence of beads–four 8/0, 1 super duo, three 8/0, 1 super duo, until you have 6 super duos with three 8/0 in between them, then end with four 8/0 beads.

Top right wire–twenty-eight 8/0 beads.

Upper wire on the right side–twenty-eight 8/0 beads.

Lower wire on the right side–sequence of beads–three 8/0, 1 super duo, three 8/0, 1 super duo, until you have 6 super duos with three 8/0 in between them, then end with four 8/0 beads.

Right wire at the bottom–sequence of beads–two 8/0, 1 super duo, three 8/0, 1 super duo, until you have 7 super duos with three 8/0 in between them, then end with two 8/0 beads.

Left wire at the bottom–twenty-eight 8/0 beads.

Lower wire on the left side–twenty-eight 8/0 beads.

Upper wire on the left side–one 8/0, 1 super duo, three 8/0, 1 super duo, until you have 7 super duos with three 8/0 in between them, then end with two 8/0 beads.

Step 3

Start braiding with the beads. Move the wire from slit 32 to slit 18. Drop one bead down toward the center of the disk. Move the wire from slit 16 to slit 2. Drop one bead down and make sure it stays at the center. Move the wire from slit 8 to slit 26. Release one bead and let it move to the center and tuck it under. Move the wire from slit 24 to slit 10. Put one bead in the center. Move the wire from slit 17 to slit 3. Drop one bead in the center. Move the wire from slit 1 to slit 19. Again drop a bead in the center.

Continue doing this until all the beads have been dropped into the center and none of the beads are left on the wires.

Step 4

Make a 1 to 2 cm long plain braid with only the wires. Secure the wires by tying knots using opposite pairs of wires one after the other and tighten the knots. Make a double knot with the last pair of wires so that the knots do not open.

Remove the braid from the disk. Prepare the ends of the braid. Cut off the excess wire.

You will see that there are 8/0 beads all around the braid and there are only two rows of super duos, which are almost on the same side with some space in between. They will be used for wrapping around the cabochon. The cabochon will be sitting in the middle of the two rows of super duos. There will be one row of super duos in front of it and another row will be behind the cabochon.

Step 5

Thread the beading needle. The thread should be around an arm's length. Put a knot at the end of the thread. This knot should be made nicely because it is going to be like a stopper so that the thread does not get pulled through the braid.

Put the needle in and out of the braid at one end and attach it to the braid. Then put the needle into the braid and take it out where the beads start.

Step 6

Go between the beads and reach the first super duo. Make the thread come out right in front of the super duo. Go through the inner hole of the super duo and make the needle come out toward the end of the braid. Then turn and put your needle through the outer hole of the super duo toward the main part of the braid.

Take out some 15/0 seeds. Pick up four beads with the needle and string them through the thread putting the needle into the outer hole of the next super duo. Keep picking four-four beads and threading them through the outer holes of all the super duos one after the other. When you reach the middle super duo add only three beads on either side of it. This will help to curve the braid in the center. After you cross the midpoint, start putting four beads between the super duos like you did earlier.

After putting the needle through the last super duo pick three beads, one super duo, and three beads with the needle and put the needle through the outer hole of the first super duo and as many beads and super duos as you can put your needle through. Then go through all the other super duos and beads once again and reach the first super duo. Go through the first super duo once again and pull the thread tightly so that the braid becomes into an oval shape.

Put the needle through the bottom hole of the first super duo and move through the beads toward the last bead at the end of the braid.

Step 7

Take out some 8/0 beads. Put the needle through this last bead, pick up one 8/0 bead, and once again put the needle through the last bead. So now both the beads will sit next to each other. Pull the thread tight. Then put the needle through the bead that you have just added. After that, put the needle through the bead that is just opposite to it at the other end of the braid. Go back through the middle bead that you added. Go through the three beads a few times to make them stay in position.

Go down through the middle 8/0 once again, pick one 8/0 bead and put the needle from the left to the right of the super duo that is still loose. Again pick one 8/0 bead and put the needle in the other 8/0 bead that is in the braid. Take your thread through these set of beads and super duo several times so that they become secure.

Step 8

Put the cabochon on this. Till now you have been working on the backside of the earring where the cabochon will be placed. Take the needle through the braid to the other side where you have to work.

Repeat step 6 on this side. But before you tighten the threads put the cabochon in the middle of the curved braid. Tighten the threads and adjust the position of the cabochon so that it fits correctly in it. See to it that none of the threads are shown. If any threads can be seen tighten them more.

Repeat step 7 and secure the cabochon. Then move your thread to one of the ends of the braid. Go through both the ends a few times and fasten them. Make a couple of knots with the thread and stitch through the ends a few more times. Cut the extra thread.

Put some glue inside the end cap and also on the ends of the braid. Cover the ends with the end cap. After the glue dries, attach the jump-rings and earring findings.

Magatama Beads

These beads are not like the other beads. They tend to be "directional" in nature. Although you can string them in a random manner and get a freeform look, you have to string them in "one direction" to get a regular pattern.

These beads "spoon" one another. When you begin to thread the magatamas you will find that you have the option to thread them "downward" or "upward." Consistency is required.

However, there is a lot of opportunity for creativity. For example, you can string the magatamas in the same direction while making a Fringe Necklace, or string them randomly when you make a bracelet.

Sometimes even though you string the magatamas correctly it may seem that they are not "spooning." If it is so, just move your hand over the magatamas from top to bottom in the direction they are slanting. This will align them correctly.

CHAPTER 11: GET A PATINA FINISH ON
THE KUMIHIMO PROJECTS

Liver of sulfur or LOS, which is one form of potassium sulfide has a gorgeous effect on copper. It helps to bring out the textural details of metal jewelry and gives them an antique look. LOS has been traditionally available as lumps in airtight metal canisters. But you can also get it in the form of liquid or gel.

It is easy to use it as a gel, and it has better results. If you use the liquid, you may use too much of it and some amount may be wasted. In case you use the LOS lump, you should use just a tiny piece, maybe as big as half of one green pea. Mix it with one-fourth cup of water and make a solution.

LOS deteriorates in sunlight. Therefore, when you make a batch cover it tightly and keep it in a cool, dark place. Moreover, see to it that there are no tools or acids near it.

Things to do Before Applying Liver of Sulfur

The metal you are going to apply LOS should have some "tooth." Although LOS can be applied on polished surfaces, it is best to have a metal that has a lightly sanded or textured finish because a highly polished surface may need several applications.

So, you can rub the pieces with 9 grit or 15 grit Finishing Films and then clean them with water and keep them aside. Then use a soft #5 watercolor brush to apply the liver of sulfur. Do not use the brush that you use for LOS application for any other purpose. Besides this, you should wear safety glasses and rubber gloves so that the chemical does not go into your eyes or touch your skin. Make sure that you keep this stuff away from all eatables and, of course, children and pets.

Techniques for Applying Liver of Sulfur

There are different ways of applying LOS. You can experiment and find the method that is most suitable for you.

Application usually depends on the type of finish that you desire. Here are some useful tips:

- If you wish to give the object a yellowish silver color dissolve a little bit of LOS gel or lump in cold water, in a glass container.
- When you apply the LOS solution, different colors will appear at various stages. First there will be yellow, then magenta, then purple and finally dark blue. You should watch carefully because these changes may occur rapidly.
- If you want the colors to be more vivid you can add a drop of detergent and a little ammonia.
- You can add an iron tablet to get a rich blue color.
- As soon as you get the desired color, dip the object in cold water. This will help the color to get set.

Another technique of application comprises of running hot water on the object and then dipping it in a glass container that has LOS in it, or using a paintbrush and painting the LOS on the areas that you want. This gives a gray or black finish.

After Applying It

You can experiment and have fun because there are a number of ways you can remove liver of sulfur if you are not satisfied with the appearance of the object.

Some of the ways in which you can get rid of it are:

- Placing the object in some warm pickle juice. Let it remain there for a few hours.
- Heating with one torch.
- By sanding.

After that, you can apply LOS once again and try to get the desired finish.

CHAPTER 12: KUMIHIMO CALCULATIONS

When you are calculating how much wire to get for your project, remember that it is always better to have a little more than the actual length.

A general rule is that you should multiply the final length of the item that you are planning to make by three to get the length of one wire that is going to be used. So the length of each wire is determined by the 3:1 ratio. For example, if the final length of the item is 20 inches the length of each wire that is going to be used in the pattern will be 60 inches.

Moreover, you have to use at least eight pieces of wire for any pattern. So you should multiply the length of that one wire by eight while calculating the length of the wire that you have to buy. In this example, it will be 60 inches multiplied by eight.

If you are going to use more than eight wires in the pattern, you should multiply the length of that one wire by that number.

Besides this, you should have some extra length of wire for knotting and doing the finishing part.

If you are planning to use beads in your project then you may need a little longer wire.

So you must keep these points in mind when calculating the length of the wire to be bought.

Conversion Chart

Here is a conversion chart to help you to determine the number of beads that are required when you use all eight bobbins.

1. Size of the bead: 6/0

   - Beads per inch: 45
   - Beads per gram: 12/g

2. Size of the bead: 8/0

   - Beads per inch: 57
   - Beads per gram: 40/g

3. Size of the bead: 11/0

   - Beads per inch: 69
   - Beads per gram: 100/g

4. Size of the bead: Delica 8

   - Beads per inch: 49
   - Beads per gram: 30/g

5. Size of the bead: Delica 11

- Beads per inch: 89
- Beads per gram: 195/g

On this basis, you can decide the number of bags (if each bag contains 8 grams) of beads to buy for your Kumihimo project.

Calculating the Number of Beads

If you are planning to use beads on eight bobbins:

- To calculate the gram weight, you should multiply the final length of the braid by the number of beads/inch.
- Then divide the answer that you get by beads/gram.
- To calculate the number of bags that you will need, divide gram weight (if each bag contains 8 grams) by eight.

For example, if you are planning to use 6/0 size beads to make a piece that is six inches long the calculation will be as follows:

- 6 (final length of the braid)* 45 (according to the chart beads/inch for beads of 6/0 size) is equal to 270
- 270 divided by 12 (according to the chart beads/gram for beads of 6/0 size) is equal to 22.5
- Then 22.5 divided by 8 is equal to 2.8

Therefore you will require three bags (if each bag contains 8 grams) of beads.

If you are planning to use beads on just a few selected bobbins:

In this case, first you must find out how many beads you need per bobbin. You can calculate in the following manner:

- If beads/inch is divided by eight bobbins it gives the number of beads/bobbin
- bead/bobbin * how many bobbins are going to have beads is equal to beads/inch
- beads/inch * final length of braid will show you how many beads you need

For example, if you are planning to use 6/0 size beads on four bobbins to make a piece that is six inches long, the calculation will be as follows:

- 45 (according to the chart number of beads/inch for 6/0 size beads) divided by 8 is equal to 5.625 (that is beads/bobbin)
- Then 5.625 (that is beads/bobbin) multiplied by 4 (the bobbins that are going to have beads) is equal to 22.5 (that is beads/inch)
- Then 22.5 (that is beads/inch) multiplied by 6 (final length of the braid) is equal to 135 (total beads

needed)

- Then 135 (total beads needed) divided by 12 (beads/gram for 6/0 size beads) is equal to 11.25 g
- 11.25 g divided by 8 is equal to 1.4

Therefore, you will require two bags (if each bag contains 8 grams) of beads.

How to Avoid Doing the Calculations

An Easy Method of Counting

If you have an Apple iPod or iPhone you can use "StitchMinder" to help you in counting when making your project. It is a stitch counting application that offers four counters. They can be customized to track pattern rows, decreases, increases, and rows completed. You can configure the counters to count downward or upward. The counts are stored by the program. So even if there is some interruption the counts are still available.

A Simple Method to Avoid Counting Beads Repeatedly

If you are using beads of the same color, you can use this method and save time as you do not need to count again and again.

For example, to make a particular pattern you may be required to string 50 beads on each wire. The beads may be so tiny that you cannot even see their hole. You may wonder how to count so many beads. It may be a strenuous task. You may need to switch on more lights or put on your reading glasses.

Instead of this, you can take a wire and count, and put on 50 beads. After that, you can use one measuring tape to measure how much space the beads occupy. In this example, the length of wire occupied by 50 beads happens to be about four inches. So, for the other wires you can measure and string beads on just four inches of wire. This will be much easier than trying to count all the beads on all the wires.

Refer to Previous Work

If you want to avoid doing the math again and again you should take notes whenever you do a Kumihimo project. Note down the length of the object you make and the length of the wire you use, the number of beads that you use for a certain pattern, and any other calculations that may be handy later.

The next time you make a project, you will have ready information from your own experience. There will be no need to do the complex calculations again and there will be fewer chances of making a mistake.

Make a Sample

Another way to avoid doing complicated calculations is to make one sample. For example, you can cut eight strands of 12 inches each. Then string eight beads into each of the wires according to your desired pattern.

So, you will use eight multiplied by eight is equal to 64 beads. You know that these beads weigh 4 grams. After using all this, you could make a braid that's one inch long. On the basis of this sample, you can estimate the amount of wire and beads that you need.

CHAPTER 13: MAKING A KUMIHIMO BRACELET

Bracelets can be found in all sizes and shapes. Some of them are thick, some flat, some of them are designed to fit tightly against the wrist while others are a bit looser. Bracelet sizing has to be more precise compared to a necklace. If there is a difference of half an inch in one necklace it does not matter. But when making a bracelet, measurements are very important.

There are several charts that can be referred for sizing bracelets. For example:

Bracelet sizes for women - Length

- Plus size - 9 inches
- Large size - 8.5 inches
- Medium size - 7.5 to 8 inches
- Small size - 7 inches

If you want to make it according to exact measurements, you can measure the wrist before making the bracelet.

You can measure using a measuring tape or wrap something flexible around the wrist and note the measurements. Paper will work if there's no measuring tape available.

Think whether you would like it to be tight or loose, and take the pattern into consideration. Add some extra length to the wrist measurement if needed and decide the finished length of the bracelet.

You should also consider the type of wire and the beads that you are going to use for the bracelet. If the wire is thick and the beads are chunky, the bracelet's inner circumference will be smaller, so you will have to make a longer bracelet.

After you know the finished length of the bracelet you should also consider how much length will be added after putting on the end cap. For this, you can measure the ending caps and minus the length of the hollow area in the caps (as the braids will go into them).

Things You Will Need

- Round Kumihimo disk
- 26 gauge soft copper wire
- 6 mm clasps and 1 or 2 jump rings
- E6000 Jewelry and Bead Adhesive
- Nylon jaw pliers
- Mandrel cone
- Some kind of weight or a small bag full of pennies.

Instructions

Step 1

Cut eight pieces of wire. They should be three times the length of the final bracelet. Put their ends together and turn them and secure them like a knot. Place this knot in the central hole of the disk.

Step 2

Hold the knot below the disk with your fingers and arrange the wires on the disk in such a manner that there is one-one wire on either side of the black positioning dots on all four sides.

That means the wires should be in slits 1 and 32 in the north, slits 16 and 17 in the south, slits 8 and 9 in the east, and slits 24 and 25 in the west.

Step 3

Move the wire from slit 1 to slit 23. Move the wire from slit 32 to slit 10. Move the wire from slit 17 to slit 7. Move the wire from slit 16 to slit 26.

Now all the wires have moved to the east and west. There are no wires in the north and south.

Step 4

Move the wire from slit 25 to slit 17. Move the wire from slit 24 to slit 32. Move the wire from slit 8 to slit 16. Move the wire from slit 9 to slit 1.

Step 5

Move the wire from slit 26 to slit 25. Move the wire from slit 23 to slit 24. Move the wire from slit 7 to slit 8. Move the wire from slit 10 to slit 9.

Now there is one-one wire on either side of the black positioning dots on all sides.

Repeat the steps from 3 to 5 and continue braiding.

Step 6

Use a Mandrel cone.

If there are no measurement marks on the mandrel cone you can make them on your own. Take a long strip of scotch tape and put it lengthwise on the cone. Then use a measuring tape and measure around the cone. Mark the number of inches on the tape. For example, if you want to measure eight inches, run the measuring tape around the cone and keep moving it until you reach the place where it measures eight inches and put a mark there.

After that, you can measure your braid on it and see whether it has reached the desired length.

Step 6

If it is of the right length stop braiding and take it out of the disk. Use nylon jaw pliers to cut the extra wires.

Turn the ending part of the wires a bit and secure them. Then take some glue and apply it to the wire ends with the help of a toothpick. Also apply some glue inside the clasps.

Put the clasps on the wire ends and press them hard. You can use jump rings to adjust it for length. Put one or two jump rings on the clasp's bar end and loop end.

CHAPTER 14: SOME IMPORTANT MISTAKES
AND THEIR SOLUTIONS

Kumihimo braiding has to be done carefully and the moves have to be made diligently to make a perfect braid. Even small mistakes like missing one bead can make a lot of difference in the final outcome. Here are some mistakes that you may make when doing Kumihimo braiding and the ways you can fix them.

Missing Out a Bead

If you miss out a bead while braiding it can create "a hole" or a vacant spot in the design. The accent beads' alignment along the edge can become awry. Moreover, it can spoil the pattern entirely. For example, a person who was making a beaded petal necklace thought that he had done everything right. He was under the impression that he had strung the beads and marked the bobbins correctly. But despite all this, the beads were not lining up. When the work was checked by an expert, it was found that he had forgotten to put one bead a quarter of an inch before he started making the petals. This very simple mistake made the complete braid go wrong.

Solution

You must check the work frequently. This is very important, especially when you are using beads with your braiding. Do not be careless or lazy about checking your work because it can be very frustrating if you reach the end of the braid and realize that your work looks skewed just because you missed one bead.

Do not hesitate to check your work and braid backward if necessary, to reach the point where you have made the mistake. You must move forward only after you have fixed it. It does not take much time to open the braid and set things right then and there.

Finding the Right Place

The beginners who are learning to make the round or Kongo braid are taught that they should leave three wires in the north or top of the disk whenever they stop their work so that they know where they should resume their work.

But sometimes there may be a sudden interruption while braiding and when you return to your work you may lose your place. It may be confusing and difficult to find out what should be your next move. You may make a wrong move and spoil the entire pattern.

Solution

Learn how to read the braid. See the central part of the Kumihimo disk where all the wires intersect. This place is also referred to as the POB or point of the braid. See the "uppers" and the "lowers" to decide your next move.

For example, if the north and south wires are resting on the east and west wires, they are the uppers. The east and west wires are under them so they are the lowers. The uppers are the last wires that you have moved. So the next step will be to move the lowers.

Next time when you drop the disk you need not fret. All you have to do is pick it up and see the point of braid and note which wires are on the top. Then turn the disk so that the lowers take the north and south positions. Start braiding. Always remember that the lowers have to be moved next.

Not Maintaining the Appropriate Tension

It is very important to maintain the correct tension while doing Kumihimo with wire. If you pull the wire excessively while braiding it may damage the disk. But if you do not pull it sufficiently the result may be a loose, misshapen braid. Sometimes the entire piece may look awry.

Solution

The wires should lie closely against each other and form an even pattern for this you must put sufficient pressure on them while braiding. Make sure that whenever you move a wire you pull it enough and press it at the point of the braid where it lies over the other wires. You can use your thumb or index finger to press the wire.

You should also check your work on the back side of the disk frequently. If the wire is misshapen or loose, or if there is some other mistake, correct it before proceeding with the braiding. Make it a point to keep your fingers close to the back side of the disk and maintain a firm grip.

You can attach some weight to the central knot so that there is an appropriate tension and the braid is even. For this, you can use some kind of weight or tie a small bag full of pennies to the knot in the central hole of the disk.

Wrong Calculations

The worst thing that can happen when braiding is that you may run out of wire or beads in the middle of the project. You may be left with an incomplete project if you do not do the calculations properly before embarking on your venture.

It is very important to have sufficient supplies and cut the right lengths of wire before you begin braiding.

Solution

Do the calculations before you start making your item. Have a clear idea of the project. Know the finished length that you desire, multiply it by three. Then multiply it by the number of wires you plan to use. Basically, eight wires are used. But you may choose to use more according to the pattern you plan to make. Add some extra length for the knot and finishing part of the braid. Remember it is always good to have a longer wire that can be trimmed later than to have a short wire and an incomplete project.

Do the math, refer to the charts or the notes you have taken down from your previous projects and find the number of beads that you will need. There is nothing wrong with having some extra beads. If they are left over you can always use them in another project later.

Not Using the Right Things

In order to do Kumihimo you require some basic things like disks, bobbins, wire, clasps or end caps, adhesive, and a nylon jaw pliers.

You can use a Kumihimo disk or a plate for making the braids, but each of them is useful for particular types of braids. The same type of disk may not be suitable for all projects. The disks are of different thicknesses and diameters. The thin ones may not be suitable for strong wires. But if you are making fine jewelry with a fine gauge wire then thin ones may be appropriate.

You should choose the right gauge wire for your project. Remember that 12 gauge wire is thicker than 24 gauge wire. So, decide how fine the wire should be for your particular project. If you make a necklace with a very thick wire you may not be able to achieve the delicacy required. If you choose to make a home decor item with very fine wire it may not stand out.

While making bracelets it is very important to know the right measurements. For this you must use a mandrel cone.

If you do not use the right type of end caps, clasps and adhesive, the finishing of the braid may not be secure enough and the braid may open after some time.

Solution

Choose the right materials and tools for the project. See to it that they are compatible with the design you are planning to make.

Major Mistake

The biggest mistake that you may make while braiding with wire is that you may overlook the fact that using wire to make a braid is much different from using any other fiber. Wire is firmer compared to other materials. It needs to be handled in the proper way or else you may not get the outcome you desire.

For example:

- Unlike fiber, which can be directly used for Kumihimo, wire has to be prepared before being used for braiding. It has to be straightened and the kinks and curves have to be removed.
- When you move the wire, you should press it at the point of braid so that it lies close to the other wires. Otherwise, the braid may not come out even and may not have a proper shape.
- While braiding with wire instead of tying a knot at one end, like you generally do with fiber, it may be more convenient to join the ends with some electrical tape or fold the ends together.
- The finishing part is also different for a wire braid. Unlike fiber that you sew the end and secure it, here you have to turn the wire ends so that the braid does not unravel. Then you have to put sufficient adhesive on the braid and inside the clasp. After that, you have to put the braid inside the clasp and

press with pliers.

CONCLUSION

If you were under the impression that Kumihimo is an expensive hobby, now you know that it is not. It is not necessary to spend a lot of money and buy gold wire or sterling silver to make a gorgeous item. You can make beautiful pieces of jewelry with much cheaper wire and minimal tools.

If you thought that it is difficult to do Kumihimo with wire after reading this guide you would have realized that with practice you can easily master it. The simple tips given in this book will help you to tame the wire and mold it in the way you want it to be.

Even if you have never done braiding before and are absolutely new to this craft, you can follow the simple steps given in this book and learn how to make the classic Kumihimo braid designs like the Basic Round braid, Kongo Gumi, Edo Yatsu, Hira Yatsu Gumi and Yurugi Gumi. Then you can use these to make various items of jewelry that you can use yourself or give as gifts to your friends.

So what are you waiting for? Go ahead get the simple tools and materials and try your hand at making wire jewelry and items of home decor. Surprise your friends and relatives by showing off your extraordinary skill and offering them unique handcrafted Kumihimo items. That, too, without impinging upon your purse or spending extravagantly.

Where to Buy the Materials

Here are five links to different stores where you can buy the materials for your Kumihimo wire weaving project.

https://www.weircrafts.com/kumihimo/kumihimo-wire.html

https://www.interweave.com/article/beading/basic-kumihimo-supplies-what-do-i-need-for-kumihimo/

https://www.whatabraid.com/pages/kumihimo-tips-hints

https://www.artbeads.com/design-studio/kumihimo-getting-started/

https://createwhimsy.com/projects/how-to-do-kumihimo-with-beads/

LEAVE A REVIEW?

Throughout the process of writing this book, I have tried to put down as much value and knowledge for the reader as possible. Some things I knew some others I spent the time to research. I hope you found this book to be of benefit to you.

If you liked the book, would you consider leaving a quick review for it? It would really help my book, and I would be grateful to you for letting other people know that you like it.

Yours Sincerely,

Amy Lange

BIBLIOGRAPHY

12 strand Yurugi -gumi. Retrieved from

https://www.youtube.com/watch?v=dhpOZez7Dg4&list=PLlrjOezwxaja0li36NZ3SFvDHQn-cXfjI&index=13&t=0s

Beaded kumihimo cabochon earrings. Retrieved from

https://www.youtube.com/watch?v=X5LvVtc0aZA

Blaine, C. (n.d.). How to do kumihimo with beads. Retrieved from

https://createwhimsy.com/projects/how-to-do-kumihimo-with-beads/

Bogert, K. (2019, April 15). Kumihimo wirework: 4 Quick tips for braiding with wire. Retrieved from

https://www.interweave.com/article/beading/kumihimo-wirework-made-easy-4-quick-tips-for-braiding-with-wire/?fbclid=IwAR3YFlpTh6BkuwmmJ8oAjyBSo4vLytRGT2661JZSfAFkBhoUXMuVy0QA7u8

Butler, J. (2018, September 24). Kumihimo wirework made easy: Techniques for perfecting braid structures. Retrieved from

https://www.interweave.com/article/jewelry/kumihimo-wirework-made-easy-techniques-for-perfecting-braid-structures/

Erickson, L. (2012, October 8). Liver of Sulfur: Create Patina on silver and copper jewelry. Retrieved from

https://www.interweave.com/article/jewelry/liver-of-sulfur-101-what-is-it-how-to-use-it-to-create-patina-on-silver-and-copper-jewelry/

Flat wire kumihimo braid. Retrieved from

https://www.youtube.com/watch?v=UvbYdX31lE0&list=PLlrjOezwxaja0li36NZ3SFvDHQn-cXfjI&index=12&t=0s

Getting started with Kumihimo. Retrieved from

https://www.artbeads.com/design-studio/kumihimo-getting-started/

How to do flat Kumihimo. Retrieved from

https://www.artbeads.com/design-studio/flat-kumihimo-braid-handy-tip/

Huntoon, K. (n.d.). Kumihimo tips & hints. Retrieved from

https://www.whatabraid.com/pages/kumihimo-tips-hints

Kumihimo conversion chart. Retrieved from

https://www.artbeads.com/artbeads-guide/artbeads-guide/2017/04/04/kumihimo-conversion-chart

Redmond, N. (n.d.). Braiding disk instructions. Kumihimo tutorials for making round braids on a braiding disk. Retrieved from

https://www.weircrafts.com/kumihimo/kumihimo-instructions/kumihimo-disk-instructions/spiral-braid.html

Redmond, N. (n.d.). Braiding disk instructions. Kumihimo tutorials for making round braids on a braiding disk. Retrieved from

https://www.weircrafts.com/kumihimo/kumihimo-instructions/kumihimo-disk-instructions/checker-braid.html

VanBenschoten, J. (2014, February 5). Basic Kumihimo supplies - What do I need for Kumihimo? Retrieved from

https://www.interweave.com/article/beading/basic-kumihimo-supplies-what-do-i-need-for-kumihimo/